Garry McQuinn
and
Amanda Faber
present

THE TWO WORLDS
OF CHARLIE F.

by Owen Sheers

Based on an original concept by Alice Driver
Directed by Stephen Rayne

First performed at Theatre Royal Haymarket
22nd January 2012

The 2014 tour is dedicated to Jack Davies,
one of the original cast members of
The Two Worlds of Charlie F.
who died in 2013 aged 23.

Supported using public funding by
**ARTS COUNCIL
ENGLAND**
LOTTERY FUNDED

In December 2010, producer Alice Driver decided to create the first theatre project for wounded, injured and sick (WIS) service personnel, bringing together the different worlds of theatre and the military, delivered through a partnership between the Theatre Royal Haymarket Masterclass Trust, The Royal British Legion and Defence Recovery Capability. The goal was to create a company of 30 WIS Service personnel and develop a new play based on their experiences, then rehearse, market, design and perform this at the Theatre Royal Haymarket in January 2012 under the guidance of a professional team.

An astonishing reaction to the first two performances led to more. This time critics attended and the play was awarded four- and five-star reviews in the national press. The reaction was so strong that The Royal British Legion agreed to fund a UK tour from June to September 2012. After 17 performances to standing ovations and sell-out audiences, the tour reached its climax when the play was awarded an Amnesty International Freedom of Expression Award.

Two of the people in the final audience were producers Garry McQuinn and Amanda Faber. They were invited by Alice Driver, Stephen Rayne and Owen Sheers to join with them to launch the second run of the play. This new tour is the product of that collaboration. It opened in February 2014 at the Princess of Wales Theatre in Toronto, Canada, by kind invitation of the Mirvish family and was followed by a UK tour.

Cast

Gareth Crabbe	Bombardier Darren Sobey
Stewart Hill	Major Daniel Thomas
Cassidy Little	Corporal Charlie Fowler
Daniel Shaw	Rifleman Leroy Jenkins
Stephen Shaw	Corporal Roger Smith
Maurilla Simpson	Lance Corporal Simi Yates
Darren Swift	Colour Sergeant Chris Ward
Ashliegh Young	Sergeant Ali Briggs
Teri Ann Bobb-Baxter	Young Simi Yates, Michelle Taylor
Tom Colley	Sapper John Booth
Miriam Cooper	Sarah Thomas, Tracy Booth, Marie Ward
Tomos Eames	Corporal Frank Taylor
Venetia Maitland	Sergeant Jean Barker
Owen Oldroyd	Captain David Philips
Lily Phillips	Lauren Preston

All other parts played by members of the ensemble

Creatives and Production

Writer   Owen Sheers
Director   Stephen Rayne
Producer   Garry McQuinn
Producer   Amanda Faber
Original Producer and Executive Producer   Alice Driver
Composer   Jason Carr
Set and Costume Designer   Anthony Lamble
Lighting and Projection Designer   William Reynolds
Sound Designer   Colin Pink
Choreographer   Lily Phillips
Costume Supervisor   Kat Smith
Costume Assistant   Danielle Gallagher

Production Manager   Alex Weller
Company Stage Manager   Matthew Hales
Deputy Stage Manager   Nick Hayman
Assistant Stage Manager   Isabelle Taylor
Assistant Production Manager   Chloe Brown Coe
Production Electrician   Neill Pollard
Production Sound Engineer   Andy Johnstone
Financial Controller   Collin Hinds
Associate Producer   Brendan Riding
Associate Producer   Owen Sheers
Assistant Producer (*Funding*)   Chloe French
Assistant Producer   Hannah Durose

Projection footage   Courtesy of Uppercut Films
Sound and Projection Equipment   Pressure Wave Audio Ltd.
Programme design   N9 Design

Marketing   JHI-marketing.com:
Jo Hutchison, Natalie Yalden, Nicole Samuels

Press   Amanda Malpass PR:
Amanda Malpass, Georgia Edmonds, Alison Duguid, Ruth Moloney

Tour Booking   Kayte Potter of Great Leap Forward
Kayte@greatleapforward.co.uk

Accountants   Shipleys: Stewart Jell, Mark Wadsworth

Legal   Pitmans: Jeremy Summers, Alan Hunt
Davenport Lyons: Paul Toolan

Mirvish Productions
David Mirvish, Brian Sewell, John Karastamatis,
David Mucci, Sue Toth, Randy Alldread, Charles Chu,
Sarah Sisko, Chris Dorscht, Michael Taylor

The Charlie F Company
Service Personnel

From sharing their stories for the script to administration, marketing and performing, wounded, injured and sick Service Personnel have contributed to *The Two Worlds of Charlie F* in a variety of ways. We are delighted to have worked with the following individuals:

Sergeant Aaron Baillie

Corporal Philip Bartlett

Marine Alex Brewer

Rifleman Billy Brumfield

Marine LCpl JJ Chalmers

Sapper Lyndon Chatting Walters

Staff Sergeant Elaine Corner

Bombardier Gareth Crabbe

Guardsman Jack Davies

Lieutenant-Colonel Stewart Hill

Guardsman Musa Jarju

Major Adam Jones

Lance Corporal Kevin Juka

Corporal Diane Lee

Lance Corporal Cassidy Little

Marine Simon Maxwell

Marine Steve Mculley

Corporal Lee Millar

Corporal Ralph Murombe

Lance Corporal Daniel O'Callaghan

Captain Ed Orr

Captain Anna Poole

Marine Eddy Porter

Guardsman Andy Pullin

Lance Bombardier Matthew Richardson

Rifleman Daniel Shaw

Corporal Stephen Shaw

Lance Corporal Maurillia Simpson

Corporal Kevin Smith

Darren Swift

Marine Ash Swinard

Liam Thompson

Corporal Paul Vice

Marine Matt Webb

Rifleman Lyndon Woodford

Private Andrew Wright

Lance Corporal Ashliegh Young

Biographies

BOMBARDIER GARETH 'CRABBIE' CRABBE
Bombardier Darren Sobey

Gareth was a Bombardier in the Royal Artillery based in Larkhill, Salisbury, before he was medically discharged from the military. He has served in Bosnia, Kosovo and Iraq. He was injured in 2007 whilst on exercise commanding a 105mm light gun, which left him needing spinal disc replacement. He is delighted to be part of *Charlie F* once again and is eager to get on the road.

LIEUTENANT COLONEL (RETIRED) STEWART (BENNY) HILL
Major Daniel Thomas, British Officer in Hospital

Stewart commissioned into the Royal Regiment of Wales in 1995. He served in the UK, Germany, Bosnia, Kosovo, Northern Ireland and two tours in Afghanistan. On 4th July 2009, Stewart was leading one hundred and sixty men in a close-combat fight against the Taliban in some of the fiercest fighting seen by UK forces in Afghanistan when shrapnel from an Improvised Explosive Device (IED) tore into his brain. Promoted to Lieutenant Colonel, he was unable to take command of his battalion due to his brain injury. He was destined for high-level promotion but was medically discharged in March 2012 having never commanded soldiers again since his injury. His life has improved significantly since being in the original production of *The Two Worlds of Charlie F*, and this experience helped him regain his motivation, desire and appreciation of life. He joined *Charlie F* because he wants to relive the joy of theatre and see how much he can push his boundaries. His brain impairments fundamentally restrict what he can do in 'work' terms as his brain's capacity to engage in productive thinking is severely reduced. Stewart has taken up artistic painting as a new, unexpected and hopeful career. He finds it magical, therapeutic and exciting and his artwork is available to buy after the show. www.stewarthill.co.uk

MARINE CASSIDY LITTLE
Corporal Charlie Fowler

Cassidy is a Royal Marine serving with 42 Commando, RM, Bickleigh Barracks, Plymouth. He was injured in Afghanistan in 2011 by an IED; these injuries extended to his lower limbs, pelvis and his left eye. He is currently going through rehabilitation at Headley Court. Cassidy is from Newfoundland, Canada. He was attracted to *Charlie F* because he has always had a lust for the stage. This project has given him something to pour his heart and soul into, a goal of which he is most proud. It has given him something to strive for and by being part of the forthcoming tour he can continue to focus on the future. He plans to continue his new career as an actor and has already appeared in a BBC drama. He also carried the Olympic Torch through Peterborough.

RIFLEMAN (RETIRED) DANIEL 'SHAWTY' SHAW
Rifleman Leroy Jenkins

Dan was a soldier in the Infantry (The Rifles) before he was medically discharged. He used to be a machine-gunner of an eight-man section. Whilst serving in Afghanistan in 2009 he lost both his legs in an IED explosion as he went to the aid of a colleague in his platoon. He now lives in Milton Keynes. His participation in the production has helped him to become even more outgoing and full of energy and he has now made a decision to pursue a career in acting. He is also designing and writing his own Anime about a double amputee with special powers.

CORPORAL (RETIRED) STEPHEN 'SANDY' SHAW
Corporal Roger Smith, Understudy: Bombardier Darren Sobey

Steve was in the Princess of Wales's Royal Regiment, before he was medically discharged from the military. He had an accident whilst driving a Snatch in Afghanistan which rolled into a canal, resulting in a fractured lower spine and neck injuries. He is now being rehabilitated in Worthing and is currently awaiting further surgery. He is very excited to be returning to *Charlie F* for its Canadian and UK tour.

LANCE CORPORAL (RETIRED) MAURILLIA 'SIMI' SIMPSON
Lance Corporal Simi Yates

Simi is originally from Trinidad and Tobago. She has recently been medically discharged from the Royal Logistic Corps as a Driver Radio Communications Specialist, and served in Iraq three times. Her leg was injured in 2010 when she was stationed in Germany whilst cycling to work. She has been rehabilitating at Headley Court. She always dreamed of joining the army and was inspired to come to England aged seven after she saw the Queen on a state visit. She lived her dream for thirteen years in the Royal Logistics Corp. She believes that being able to live your dream is a privilege and a gift, not to be taken for granted but to be cherished for a lifetime. Since performing on stage she achieved a place in the Paralympics Reserve Volleyball team. Now she has been selected for the GB Sitting Voleyball team with the dream of success to carry on the London legacy of 2012 to Rio in 2016.

DARREN SWIFT 'SWIFTY'
Colour Sergeant Chris Ward,
Understudy: Rifleman Leroy Jenkins, Sergeant Ali Briggs.

Swifty joined the Army (Royal Green Jackets, now 2 Rifles) in 1982 after leaving school at 16 and during his third tour of Northern Ireland was involved in a terrorist attack resulting in the loss of his legs and various other injuries. After being medically discharged from the Armed Forces in 1992, he has been working as a Film and TV Supporting Artist / Action Performer and as a Trauma Casualty Amputee for the Military and the Civilian Emergency Services. He has performed and toured with the National Theatre's production of *Travelling Light*. He has participated in adventurous expeditions and sports including skiing and snowboarding, canoeing, rafting, skydiving, hand-cycling and climbing, and mentors for the Not Forgotten Association, which is a unique national tri-service charity which provides entertainment, leisure and recreation for the serving wounded, injured or sick and for ex-service men and women with disabilities. Although originally from London he now lives with his wife Sarah and daughter Isabelle in the Lake District.

LANCE CORPORAL ASHLIEGH 'BIG ASH' YOUNG
Sergeant Ali Briggs, Understudy: Colour Sergeant Chris Ward

Ash is in the Royal Logistic Corps and was formerly in the Royal Anglian Regiment. He has served in Iraq, Northern Ireland and Germany. He suffered leg damage in 2006, whilst on a machine-gun run and is currently rehabilitating in Peterborough. He was attracted to the *Charlie F* project because he thought it was something new. Since performing in January, Ash has spent time in the Battle Back Centre Project training in Adaptive Sports at Lilleshall and has also completed a work placement at Barclays Bank.

TERI ANN BOBB-BAXTER
Young Simi Yates, Michelle Taylor, Nurse, Dancer 2, Ensemble,
Understudy: Lance Corporal Simi Yates

Teri trained at the Arts Educational Schools London, graduating with a BA Hons in Acting. Theatre includes: *#I Am England* (Talawa Theatre Company at Sadler's Wells), *The Day the Waters Came* (Theatre Centre), *Dancing Dog Gets a Credit Card* (Soho Theatre). Workshops include: Sylv in *East* Masterclass with Linda Marlowe (Theatre Royal Haymarket). Roles whilst in training include: Victoria in *Victoria*, Ophelia in *Hamlet*. Teri is delighted to be making her touring debut with *The Two Worlds of Charlie F*.

TOM COLLEY
Sapper John Booth, Understudy: Corporal Frank Taylor, Corporal Roger Smith, Captain David Philips, Businessman 1

Tom trained at Central School of Speech and Drama. Theatre credits include *The Judas Kiss* (Hampstead Theatre, UK tour, Duke of York Theatre), *As Is* (Finborough Theatre), *The Wind in the Willows* (Theatre 503), *Othello, Hippolytus, Ajax, Antigone* (international tours with Altitude North Theatre Company). Film and television work includes *Call the Midwife, The Silver Goat, The Proxy, Salting the Battlefields* and *The Truth About Stanley.*

MIRIAM COOPER
Sarah Thomas, Tracy Booth, Nurse Marie Ward, Ensemble, Understudy: Psychologist

Miriam trained at the Guildford School of Acting. Her theatre work ranges from the Bristol Old Vic in *The Ghost Train* to London's Young Vic in Ibsens *Playing with Fire.* She was most recently seen in London as Elizabeth and Mary in her one woman show *Prostitutes Marry in May*, where she received an Off West End Theatre Awards nomination for best female performer. Other notable roles include Shakespeare's Lady Macbeth (UK tour), Kate Mundy in *Dancing at Lughnasa* (Lancaster Dukes Playhouse), Flora in *A Slight Ache* and Sarah in *The Lover* by Harold Pinter (European Arts Company), Juliet Margaret Cameron, the 19th Century Photographer for BBC Radio 4 and Mary Anning, *The Fossil Hunter* for the BBC.

She has written, directed and performed for Play on Words Theatre, for whom she is a director. www.miriamcooper.co.uk

TOMOS EAMES
Corporal Frank Taylor, Businessman 2, Understudy: Corporal Charlie Fowler, Sapper John Booth

Tomos Eames was born in Cardiff and is a fluent Welsh speaker. He attended the three-year acting course at the Central School of Speech and Drama, also training through a summer exchange project in the MXAT Moscow.

Theatre credits include: *Trwy'r Ddinas Hon* (Sherman Theatre Wales), *Rape of The Fair Country* (Theatre Clwyd) *Spirit of the Mimmosa* (Theatre Clwyd) *Deffro'r Gwanwyn* (Theatre genedlaethol Cymru)

Film credits include: *Resistance* (Resistance Films), *Say Nothing* (short), *Pride*, Proud Productions and *The Best Possible Taste* BBC.

Television credits include: *Siblings* for the BBC and *Gwaith Cartref for* S4C.

VENETIA MAITLAND
Sergeant Jean Barker, Waitress, Ensemble,
Understudy: Nurse, Dancers 1 and 2, Lauren Preston,
Tracy Booth, Acting Assistant Stage Manager

After graduating from The University of Exeter where she studied drama, Venetia trained at The Oxford School of Drama. Her work in theatre includes *A Midsummer Night's Dream* (Blenheim Palace), *Attempts on Her Life* (Hampstead Downstairs), *To Kill a Mockingbird* (York Theatre Royal, UK Number One tour) and *Twelfth Night* (The Rose Theatre, Bankside).

In film Venetia has recently played the lead in *Ben* (directed by BAFTA winner Michael Stevenson) and *The Underwater Realm* (shot entirely underwater and directed by David M Reynolds).

She has also appeared in various audio books and radio plays for the RNIB and BBC.

OWEN OLDROYD
Captain David Philips, Psychologist, Delivery Man,
Singing Teacher, Businessman 1,
Understudy: Major Daniel Thomas, Businessman 2

Owen's theatre work includes *Mamma Mia*, Father Alex, international tour, dir. Paul Garrington, *Blood Brothers*, Narrator, WestEnd, dir. Bob Tomson/Bill Kenwright, *Blood Brothers*, Mr. Lyons, UK tour, dir. Bob Tomson/Bill Kenwright, *Don't dress for dinner*, Bernard, Jumeirah Theatre, Dubai, dir. James Horne, *Fab Four*, Paul McCartney, tour of Italy, dir. Fraser Grant, *A Midsummer Night's Dream*, Bottom, tour of Italy, dir. Fraser Grant, *Rednext and Politics*, Tony, The Pleasance, Edinburgh, dir. Will Scarnell, *The Dutch Courtesan* , Tysefew, Wimbledon Studio, dir. Alex Chisholm. Repertory seasons at Wolverhampton Grand; Taunton Brewhouse; The Gala Theatre, Durham; Middlesbrough Theatre; The Lyceum, Crewe; Queen's Theatre, Stoke.

Roles include: *Hay Fever*, Simon Bliss, dir. Howard Ross, *Abigail's Party*, Tony, dir. Howard Ross, *Taking Steps*, Tristram, dir. Hugo Myatt, *A Murder is Announced*, Patrick, dir. Howard Ross, *The Edge of Darkness*, Ivan Livago, dir. Paul Mead, *A Shred of Evidence*, Inspector Beecroft, dir. Howard Ross, *Anagram of Murder*, Det. Insp. Morgan, dir. Nick Barclay, *Wait until Dark*, Mike, Trenton, dir. Howard Ross, *Fatal Encounter*, Howard, dir. Hugo Myatt, *Private Lives*, Victor Prynne, dir. Howard Ross

His TV work includes Private Shaw in *Western Lights*, (HTV); Gala Announcer in *Dive* (BBC2) and various roles in hidden camera set-ups for *The Friday Night Project*.

On radio Owen is the voice of Chief Inspector Fang in the BBC series *The Scarifyers*.

LILY PHILLIPS
Lauren Preston, Dancer 1, Ensemble, Choreographer

Lily trained at Margaret Howard Theatre College. Lily's dance credits include: *Cabaret Dancer* (Green Room Cabaret Club), *Rolling Back the Years* (UK tour) *Twenty Twenty Live* tour (02 Academy). Lily's acting credits include: Bex in *Paper Fortunes* (Canal Cafe Theatre) and commercials for Channel 5 and Sony. Lily is also part of a comedy cabaret show *The Ruby Darlings* (Edinburgh Fringe Festival, Park Theatre), which she co-writes and performs in. Her choreography credits include *Alix* (Music Promo), *Twenty Twenty* (Music Promo Kerrang! No.1,) *A Midsummer Night's Dream* (Theatre Royal Haymarket). Lily was part of the original production of *The Two Worlds of Charlie F* as the choreographer and is very excited to be back choreographing and performing for the tour.

The Creative Team

OWEN SHEERS
Writer

Owen Sheers is the author of two poetry collections, *The Blue Book* and *Skirrid Hill* (winner of the Somerset Maugham Award). His debut prose work *The Dust Diaries* was short-listed for the Royal Society of Literature's Ondaatje Prize and won the Welsh Book of the Year 2005. In 2004 he was Writer in Residence at the Wordsworth Trust and in 2007 Owen was a Cullman Fellow at the New York Public Library. Owen's first novel, *Resistance*, won a 2008 Hospital Club Creative Award and was short-listed for the Writers Guild Best Book Award. *Resistance* is translated into ten languages and Owen co-wrote the screenplay for the film adaptation released in 2011. His oratorio with Rachel Portman, *The Water Diviner's Tale*, was premiered at the Royal Albert Hall for the BBC Proms 2007. In 2011 Owen wrote *The Passion*, National Theatre Wales' 72-hour site-specific production in Port Talbot staring and directed by Michael Sheen. Other theatrical work includes: the radio play *If I Should Go Away* and *Pink Mist*, a verse drama for BBC Radio 4 which won the Hay Poetry Medal 2013 and is published by Faber. In 2012 Owen was writer in residence for the Welsh Rugby Union. His account of the year *Calon: A Journey to the Heart of Welsh Rugby* was published by Faber in 2013.

STEPHEN RAYNE
Director

Stephen Rayne began directing at York Theatre Royal and Cambridge Theatre Company with: *Moll Flanders*; *The Comedy of Errors*; *The Rivals*; *The Can Opener*; *John Bull's Other Island*; *Pride and Prejudice*. On the West End: *Me and My Girl*; *Who Plays Wins*; *Look No Hands*; *Heartbreak House*; *Timon of Athens*; *The Seagull*. Royal Shakespeare Company: *The Plantagenets*; *Hamlet*; *The Comedy of Errors*; *They Shoot Horses, Don't They?* *The Constant Couple*; *The Great White*

Hope; Othello. Royal National Theatre as associate and co-director: *The Cherry Orchard; An Enemy of the People; Mutabilitie; The Relapse; The Coast of Utopia; Not About Nightingales* (also Broadway). As a freelance director: more than 30 productions in London and regions. Operas: *Peter Grimes, Idomeneo* (Glyndebourne); *Sophie's Choice* (Royal Opera House). Musicals: *Pajama Game; Jekyll; Lock Up Your Daughters; King and I; Gone with the Wind.* US credits: *Parade; Sabrina Fair; The Heavens are Hung in Black; A View from the Bridge; Closer; Hay Fever; Equus; House and Garden; Hamlet; Macbeth; Blood Knot; A Christmas Carol; The Civil War. International: Jesus Christ Superstar* (Spain); *Havana Rakatan.* Most recently *Our Town* (Washington) *Chantecler Tango* (Buenos Aires and Paris). *The Long Way Home* (Sydney Theatre Co.).

GARRY MCQUINN
Producer

Garry graduated from Australia's national theatre school (NIDA) and has spent the past 35 years working behind the scenes in a wide range of roles. He has mounted and produced large-scale musicals such as Disney's *Beauty and the Beast, The Boy from Oz* and *Showboat,* and the international tours of shows including *Tap Dogs, Slava's Snowshow, Mums the Word, Gumboots, Shaolin Monks of China, Matthew Bourne's Swan Lake, Circus Oz* and most notably as lead producer and managing partner for *Priscilla Queen of the Desert, the Musical. Priscilla* is the most successful Australian musical of all time. Opening in Australia in 2006, *Priscilla* ran for three years in London's West End and played to over 600,000 people on Broadway. Seasons followed in Milan, Sao Paulo, Rome, Stockholm and on tour in both the United Kingdom and North America. New productions are planned this year in Seoul, Madrid, Buenos Aires, Athens and Manila, and a return to Australia is scheduled for 2015. Garry has also produced the world premiere of Ingmar Bergman's *Through A Glass Darkly* with the Almeida Theatre in London, and with the Atlantic Theatre in New York. He is currently developing a show based on the music of Van Morrison.

AMANDA FABER
Producer

Amanda works as a producer in film, television and now theatre. In 2011 she produced *Resistance,* starring Michael Sheen and Andrea Riseborough, which was nominated for the Cine Vision Award at the Munich Film Festival and for which Sharon Morgan won a Welsh BAFTA 2012 for Best Actress. In 2012 she produced *Jadoo,* starring Kulvinder Ghir, Harish Patel, Amara Karan and Tom Mison, which premiered in offical selection at the Berlin Film Festival 2013. Before that Amanda directed and produced at the BBC in Documentaries, News and Current Affairs and General Factual before setting up her own production company. Credits include: *Breaking the Silence, Guilty my Arse, The Race for Everest, Children with a Difference, Crooked Britain* and *Watchdog.* She is a qualified teacher and solicitor and was a senior lecturer at the College of Law, London. She is founder and Chair of KINOE, a charity which helps to educate around 4,500 children in Nepal and India (www.KINOE.org).

ALICE DRIVER
Original Producer and Executive Producer

Alice has built up her experience in the West End at the Theatre Royal Haymarket. Her credits include Shakespeare's *A Midsummer Night's Dream, Run Rabbit Run*, Capek's *The Insect Play* and *Confusion, Waiting for Godot, Too Much the Sun* and *The Problem with the Seventh Year*. She also ran the Theatre Royal Haymarket Masterclass Trust and worked in the development department at the National Theatre. In business she has worked in training and development both in-house at the international recruitment agency Hydrogen and as a consultant with a range of clients. Alice set up and produced the original production and tour of *The Two Worlds of Charlie F* in partnership with the Theatre Royal Haymarket Masterclass Trust, the Royal British Legion and the Ministry of Defence. The partnership with the Royal British Legion was nominated for a Third Sector Excellence award and whilst on tour the play won the Amnesty Award for Freedom of Expression. Subsequently Alice has gone on to design and develop learning and development programmes for Great Ormond Street Hospital, Richard House Hospice, Homeless shelters and most recently has been involved in delivering training for the School of Hard Knocks. She worked with the Australian Department of Defence to support the set up of the Australian version of the model behind *The Two Worlds of Charlie F*.

ANTHONY LAMBLE
Set and Costume Designer

Anthony's theatre credits include *Shush, The Passing, The East Pier, Bookworms, The Comedy of Errors* and *The Playboy of the Western World* (Abbey Theatre); *Ciara, The Artist Man and The Mother Woman, The Arthur Conan Doyle Appreciation Society* (Traverse); *The Two Worlds of Charlie F* (Theatre Royal Haymarket/Pleasance Edinburgh); *For Once* (Pentabus); *Relatively Speaking* (Watermill); *Shivered* (Southwark); *The Complaint, Everything is Illuminated* (Hampstead); *The Price* (West End/Tricycle/Tour); *The Caucasian Chalk Circle, Translations, Sing Yer Heart Out for the Lads, A Midsummer Night's Dream, As You Like It* (National Theatre); *Measure for Measure, Richard III, The Roman Actor, King Baby* (Royal Shakespeare Company); *The Entertainer* (Old Vic), as well as numerous productions for the Royal Court, Menier Chocolate Factory, West Yorkshire Playhouse and the Bush Theatre.

Dance and opera credits include *Facing Viv* (English National Ballet), *L'Orfeo* (Japan tour), *Palace in the Sky* (English National Opera) and *Broken Fiction* (Royal Opera House).

WILLIAM REYNOLDS
Lighting Designer

William trained at the Motley Theatre Design School.

Set and lighting designs include: *Waiting and Sexing the Cherry* (Southbank Centre), *Saturday Night* (Arts Theatre), *Moonfleece* (UK tour), Schools Theatre Festival (Young Vic) and *La Boheme* (Palestine tour).

Lighting includes *Daredevas* (Southbank Centre), *Nuit d'Electronique et d'Opera* (Theatre Royal de Wallonie, Belgium), *The Magic Flute* (Palestine tour) *The Company Man* (Orange Tree Theatre). Projection designs include *Testament* (Dublin Theatre Festival), *Prima Donna* (Sadlers Wells), *The Gambler* (Royal Opera House) and *Das Rheingold* (National Reisopera, Holland).

JASON CARR
Composer

After winning the Vivian Ellis Prize for Young Writers of Musicals, Jason was invited by Peter Hall to compose the musical *Born Again* (Chichester Festival Theatre starring Mandy Patinkin and José Ferrer). As Associate Composer at Chichester, Jason wrote music and lyrics for two new musicals: *The Water Babies* and *Six Pictures of Lee Miller* (nominated for the British Composer Awards). His adaptation of *A Christmas Carol* has played Chichester, Birmingham Rep and West Yorkshire Playhouse. Jason has composed incidental music for over 50 plays, most recently providing additional music for *Chariots of Fire* (Hampstead and Gielgud).

Orchestration credits includes the Menier Chocolate Factory's *Sunday in the Park with George*, *La Cage aux Folles* and *A Little Night Music* (all also Broadway, winning Drama Desk Award and two Tony nominations for Best Orchestrations).

Jason accompanies many singers, including Dame Felicity Lott and Maria Friedman.

COLIN PINK
Sound Designer

The Guildhall School of Music and Drama. Resident at the National Theatre before freelance in theatre, live events and film. Principal Sound Consultant for 2012 Olympic Games. Theatre Designs: *The History Boys*, *The Witches Of Eastwick*, *The King and I*, Derren Brown's *Enigma* and *Svengali*, *Sweeny Todd*, *Imagine This*, *The Night Of The Iguana*, *Troilus and Cressida*, *Brassed Off*, *Closer*, *Treasure Island*, *Oliver! DreamGirls*, *Chicago*, *Guys and Dolls* and *Cabaret*.

Live Music credits: *The Classical Brit Awards*, *José Carreras*, *Plácido Domingo*, *Dame Kiri Te Kanawa*, *Herbie Hancock*, *Katherine Jenkins*, *Marti Pellow*, *BBC Concert*, *RCO* and *Dallas*.

Film credits: *Stage Beauty*, *Alfie* and *Mrs Henderson Presents*.

Who Are Our Charity Partners?

We are raising funds for our charlty partner, The Royal British Legion. This money will be spent on The Royal British Legion's Bravo 22 Company welfare project ,which uses theatre to support the recovery of wounded injured and sick service personnel, veterans, their families and the local community on a regional level. The patrons of the Bravo 22 Company are General Sir David Richards, Trevor Nunn, Ray Winstone and Alan Yentob.

The Royal British Legion stands shoulder to shoulder with all who serve. It is the nation's leading Armed Forces charity providing care and support to all members of the British Armed Forces past and present and their families. It is also the national Custodian of Remembrance and safeguards the Military Covenant between the nation and its Armed Forces. It is best known for the annual Poppy Appeal and its emblem, the red poppy.

www.britishlegion.org.uk

The Producers

are delighted to be partnering with

The Royal British Legion

Any donations kindly received will go directly to
The Bravo 22 Company project.

The producers would like to thank the following who have made this production possible

Supported using public funding by Arts Council England

Sarah Brignal, Mathew and Francesca Cadbury, Paddy and Janie Dear, Robin and Verena Fawcett, Michael Hough, Nicholas Lambert, David Larsen, Roy Martin, James Strathallan, Geoffrey H Trew, Elaine and Linus Wright

Special thanks to

Ministry of Defence

Canadian Armed Forces
Canadian Chief of Defence General Thomas J. Lawson

The Patrons of Bravo 22 Company
General Sir David Richards, Trevor Nunn, Ray Winstone and Alan Yentob.

Thanks also to

**The following corporations for their support
of Bravo 22 Company and the play**
AKA, Army and Navy Club, Brecon Beacon Cottages, Brixton St Vincents, Colombo Centre, Delfont Mackintosh Theatres, Field Fisher Waterhouse, Fiery Angel, Fitness First, The Food Show, Fraser Hamilton Printers, Friexenet, Institute of Directors, John Good Ltd, Kleinwort Benson, Marks & Spencer Plc, Naval and Military Club, Nimax Theatres Ltd, Rankin Photography, Shepherd Neame, Tesco Plc, The Third Space, Union Jack Club, Victory Services Club, Youth Hostel Association

Syndicate of Bravo 22 Company
Anonymous, Michael and Sigi Aiken, The Dewan Foundation

Donors of Bravo 22 Company
Lord and Lady Montagu of Beaulieu, Eric Gold, Sarah Willis

Theatre Royal Haymarket
Arnold M Crook, Nigel Everett and Grace Staniland

Theatre Royal Haymarket Masterclass Trust
Blayne George, Anoushka Warden, Hazel Kerr, Tom Evans

Masterclass Development Board
Patrica Acha, Fiona Arghebant, Katy Egan, William Differ, Jeanne Mandry, Becky Purves, Richard Polo, Joyce Reuben, Phyllis Walters, Fiona Williams

The Royal British Legion
Chris Simpkins, Becky Warren, Teresa Greener, Carol Smith,
Sue Freeth, Charles Bryant

Army Recovery Capability
Colonel Charlie Knaggs

Naval Service Recovery Pathway

Hasler Company

Recovery Career Services
Adrian Jackson

Rankin Photography
Rankin, Nina Rassaby-Lewis, David Allain, and everyone at the Company

Uppercut Films
Chris Terrill and Chris Hall

Nullabor Productions
Garry McQuinn, Bradley Stauffer-Kruse, Collin Hinds, Hannah Durose,
Caitlin Albery Beavan, Marine Gouverner

Thanks also to the original cast members for their contribution and support
Jamie Buller
Rob Blackwood
Sam Pearl
Sofir Stuart

We would specifically like to thank the following

Nancy Branco, Lieutenant Colonel R. M. Dorney MBE,
Elaine Hann, Colonel Fred Hargreaves, Stevan Jackson,
William and Barbara Little, Jo-Anne Macdonald, Rita and Paul Skinner,
Colonel Giles Stibbe, Kristine Tang, Commodore Mark Watson,
The Wellington Barracks

Raleigh Addington, Megan Aitken, Catriona Alderton, David Allain,
Jan Baister, Jane and NIgel Bell, Emily Bevan, Alex Baillie Hamilton,
Alice Black, Belinda Boakye, Dr Henrietta Bowden-Jones, Lisa Brooklyn,
Kanto Bzheta, Lea Carroll, Kim Canlin, Joni Carter, David Charles,
Hannah Clapham, Ben Clare, Brendan Coyle, Criterion theatre staff,
Sarah Coulton, Gavin Curtis, Natalie Cronick, Catherine and George
Davies, Archdeacon Delaney, Chloe Delevinge, Mike Driver, Kate Edge,
Idras Elba, Anna Evans, Toby Faber, Tracey Farrell, Henry Filloux-Bennett,

Anthony Fisher, Lady Fraser, Isaac Freeth, Jack Freud, Caroline Funnell, Garrick theatre staff, Gielgud theatre staff, Rina Gill, Ed Grant, Beetle Graves, Kate Green, Harry Hadden-Paton, Will Hall-Smith, Ruth Hawkins, Will Hay, Haymarket Hotel, Caprice Holdings, Annie Holcroft, Hot Brands Cool Place, Sunita Hinduja, Gloria Hunniford, Charlotte Jenkins, Helen Johnson, Helen and Charlie Keeling, Gavin Kerr, Steve King, Hannah and Jonny Kirsop, Rebecca Koczan, Gavin Kimble, Al Knight, Caz and Jonathan Knight, Sir General Graeme Lamb, LaSCoT, John Lawrie, Leeds University Alumni, The Lion in Winter Cast and Crew, Jo Lovelady, David Maas, Rowena Macey, Maia Mackney, Lucy Maitland, Sienna Miller, Lisa Mitchard, Scott Mitchell, David Morrisey, Matilda Moreton, Mousetrap Theatre Projects, Lara Nahum, Helen Nicholson, NSDF, Vince O'Brien, offwestend.com, Matthew Palin, Ruth Powell, Prince Edward theatre staff, Quintessentially, Paulette Randall, Major Trevor Rawson, Iwan Rheon, The Ritz London, Laura Rourke, Brian Russell, Danny Sapani, Ed Sargent, Helen Slater, Social Courier, SOLT, Emily and Will Shaw, Mary Stone, Mark Stradling, Howard Taylor, Patricia Tofes, Lisa Travers, Andrew Tsai, Simon Trussler, Kate Turnbull, Harriet Usher, Laura Wade-Gery, Lela Weavers, Ben Whitworth, Michael Wiggs, Charles Williams, Debbie Wilson, Becky Wootton, Barbara Windsor, Dinah Wood, David Yeates and all the wives, partners and families of the personnel involved, and to everyone who supported the production.

The Two Worlds of Charlie F.

Owen Sheers has written two collections of poetry, *The Blue Book* and *Skirrid Hill*. His non-fiction includes *The Dust Diaries* and *Calon: A Journey to the Heart of Welsh Rugby*. His novel *Resistance* has been translated into ten languages and was made into a film in 2011. His plays include *The Passion* and *The Two Worlds of Charlie F.* Owen wrote and presented BBC Four's *A Poet's Guide to Britain*. He has been a NYPL Cullman Fellow, Writer in Residence for the Wordsworth Trust and Artist in Residence for the Welsh Rugby Union.

OWEN SHEERS

The Two Worlds of Charlie F.

FABER & FABER

First published in 2012
by Faber and Faber Limited
74–77 Great Russell Street,
London WC1B 3DA

This revised edition 2014

Typeset by Country Setting, Kingsdown, Kent CT14 8ES
Printed and bound by CPI Group (UK) Ltd, Croydon CR0 4YY

A CIP record for this book
is available from the British Library

ISBN 978-0-571-31558-1

FSC
www.fsc.org
MIX
Paper from
responsible sources
FSC® C101712

2 4 6 8 10 9 7 5 3 1

Characters

Charlie Fowler
Nurse
British Officer
Charlie's Mother
Lauren Preston
David Philips
Jean Barker
John Booth
Daniel Thomas
Roger Smith
Leroy Jenkins
Chris Ward
Ali Briggs
Simi Yeats
Young Simi
Darren Sobey
Frank Taylor
Michelle
Sarah Thomas
Tracy Booth
Marie Ward
Psychologist
Singing Teacher
Delivery Man
Businessman 1
Businessman 2
Dancer 1
Dancer 2
Waitress
Common-Room Nurses

THE TWO WORLDS OF CHARLIE F.

Act One

SCENE ONE – WAKING

Footage of soldiers' boots on patrol is projected on to gauze.
  Lights fade.

Blackout.

Silence.

  The sound of an IED explosion. In its wake military radio chatter, the thudding of a helicopter, loud at first then fading down.

Charlie (*voice-over*) Your hearing's the last to go.

  The radio crackle melds into the sound of a hospital, the digital heartbeat of medical machines getting louder.

And the first to come back.

  The lights come up on a cloud of dust, still clearing from the stage. A hospital bed surrounded by screens, backlit. The silhouette of a man lying in the bed.
  A non-Caucasian nurse enters and walks behind the screens. She carries a tray with a water bottle and a glass. She, too, is silhouetted as she works. As she dresses her patient's stump he begins to stir.

Nurse What's your name?

  He stares at her, his breathing becoming rapid.

Charlie Fuck. You.

Nurse You're in Birmingham, in hospital –

Charlie / Fuck you, you Taliban bitch!

Nurse / Can you remember your name?

Charlie (*shouting*) Help! Help! I'm in here! Here!

He tries to get out of bed but fails.

Nurse You're in Selly Oak Hospital. Please, can you remember your name?

Charlie (*shouting*) ANA! ANA! ANA!

Nurse You'll wake the other patients.

Charlie Help! Radio my position! Radio my position! ANA! ANA! ANA!

Nurse Would you like some water?

Charlie ANA! AN . . . Water?

She pours a glass of water.

Oh no you don't. You're going to poison me. You think I'm fucking stupid? You're going to kill me. That's fucking cleaning fluid!

Nurse It's from a bottle.

Charlie Show me.

She opens a fresh bottle in front of him and pours it into a plastic cup. As she approaches him Charlie knocks it from her hand.

Fuck off! I'm a British soldier! Help! Over here! It was the terp wasn't it? I bet it was the fucking terp.

He begins singing 'I'm Henry the Eighth I Am!'
The Nurse exits. When she re-enters she is with an Officer in British military uniform. Both enter the screens. Charlie stops singing.

You fucking turncoat! You motherfucking traitor! I swear, when I get out of here I am going to rip out your throat, shit down your neck and wipe your fucking gene pool from the face of the earth.

The Officer nods, then leaves. Charlie returns to his song.

Nurse You're in Birmingham. In hospital. They'll move you off the ward if you carry on like this.

Charlie (*between bursts of song*) Yeah, Birmingham, of course I am. Birming-fucking-ham? I don't think so. Boss! Boss! Don't leave me in here! Don't leave me!

The Officer enters. He is with a young woman, Lauren. They both walk behind the screens.
At first Charlie doesn't see her. He continues his shouting and swearing.

Lauren Charlie? Charlie, it's me.

He turns to look at her and immediately starts crying.

Charlie Oh Jesus. Lauren, how did they get you? I swear, when I get out of here I am going to kill every motherfucking one of you. Baby, have they hurt you? Did they torture you? If you've touched one hair on her head –

Lauren, shocked, begins to leave. The Officer exits with her. He returns with an older woman, Charlie's Mother.

Charlie's Mother Charles? It's your mother. Calm down now, calm down.

Charlie Mom? No, no, not you too. No, this has to stop! Stop stop stop stop!!

The cubicle goes dark. Charlie suddenly bursts through the downstage screen, falling to the ground. He is in uniform, one leg missing, and leans on his crutch. He looks at the audience.

Charlie You know when you fell off your bike? As a kid? Do you remember that pain? The one you don't feel at first, but then you look down at your hand, your knee and it's all gritty from where you bounced along the pavement. And that's when it comes on, pulsing, and you're like, 'Ow, ow, ow, what the fuck?'

That's what I remember. That kinda feeling. Grit in my hands, my knees.

In my mouth. The taste of it.

And the smell of Afghan. Gritty and shitty. Sand, skin flakes and shit.

That's what I remember.

Beat.

I don't remember waking up.

I don't remember eating breakfast.

I don't remember being given orders, or loading up, or leaving the compound.

I don't remember going where we went.

I don't remember walking through an archway, a low archway.

I don't remember the IED going off.

None of that.

Beat.

What I *do* remember is taking down our ponchos the night before because there was a heelo coming in the next day. Then lying down in my trench on some shitty deflated air mattress and looking up at the Afghan stars which, let me tell you, are like no other fucking stars anywhere else.

Next thing I know, I'm being tortured by the fucking Taliban. For three weeks.

If anyone tries to tell you an induced coma is any kind of fun, they're fucking lying. So, yeah, I realise I must have looked like a class-A asshole back there just now, but you have to understand I wasn't in that hospital bed. Sure, I was in that bed, and as far as my fiancée and my mother were concerned I was there. Their Charlie was back. But at the same time he wasn't. That round light above me? That was an observation hole. The screens? A temporary Taliban holding station. The nurse? Some devious fucking interrogator. The pain and the tubes? That was the torture.

'I Am Henry the Eighth I Am'? No fucking idea. Didn't even know that song had more than two lines.

Beat.

When British soldiers were wounded in the Napoleonic wars it took them months to get home, if they did. In World War One a fortnight at least. World War Two, about the same from France, much longer from India, Egypt, Burma. Now? Medevaced from Nad Ali north to Bastion in twenty minutes, back in the UK in twelve, thirteen hours tops. But in here –

He taps his head.

Even quicker than that. Pretty much insta-fucking-taneous. Blink-of-an-eye kinda stuff. With a few weeks' high-definition hallucinations thrown in for free.

The only problem is that when you come back that quick not all of you comes back at once.

He lifts up his stump.

And I don't mean the fucking obvious either.

Beat.

There was this one time, on Herrick Five. I was out on patrol. Sangin. Some kids came up. They were talking to one of the ANA soldiers. I asked him what they wanted.

13

He said, 'They want to know where you are from?'
I said, 'Tell them the other side of the world.' So he did.
But then the terp started laughing. I asked him what was
so funny. He said, 'He told them you were from another
world.'

At the time I told the terp to correct him. But now,
well, I kinda think he might have had it right the first
time round.

Beat.

Before we get any further I can see more than one of you
out there are thinking, 'What kind of an accent is that
for a *Royal* Marine anyway?' Well, I'll tell you, my
friends. Canadian, that's what, and don't you fucking
forget it. Or the Fijians, the Trinidadians, the Gambians,
the Gurkhas. Oh yeah, thanks to your over-industrious
forebears we're all in this Afghan shit together, all us
citizens of the Commonwealth.

And now, for the brief time *we* have together, so are
you. So, shall we get started?

He throws a wide smile.

Let's go on a tour.

SCENE TWO – HISTORIES

Charlie stands to attention.

Charlie PO56085M.
    Cpl Charlie Fowler.
    Aged twenty-eight.
    B company 22 commando, Royal Marines.
    Injured in Nad Ali North, September 23rd 2011.
    I was on a Section assault on a compound when a
western flank stepped on an IED. Op was successful.
Casevaced from the area to Bastion and then to Selly
Oak Hospital, UK. After three weeks in a medically

induced coma, I spent four weeks at QE, then straight to
Headley Court.

*Halfway through his speech Charlie is joined on stage
by Leroy, who also begins reciting his history as
Charlie continues his at a lower volume. This pattern
is repeated with each soldier entering earlier and
earlier in the previous soldier's speech until the stage is
filled with wounded soldiers reciting their histories.*

Leroy 25044898.
Rifleman Leroy Jenkins.
Aged twenty-two.
4th Batt, The Rifles.
Injured on 26th July 2009, Helmand Province,
Afghanistan.
Left leg blown off in an IED strike, medevaced back to
the UK.
Recovery in Selly Oak Hospital Birmingham for eight
weeks. Right leg amputated. Rehab at Headley Court for
a year. Awaiting medical discharge at Tedworth House.

Daniel 542711.
Major Daniel Thomas.
Aged thirty-nine.
2nd Battalion, Royal Welsh.
Suffered a traumatic brain injury in an IED strike
whilst commanding a company on 4th July 2009 in
Babaji, Afghanistan.
Medevaced to Bastion, Khandahar, Queen Elizabeth
Hospital, Birmingham.
Discharged after six weeks.
Spent seven months in Headley Court for Brain
Rehabilitation. Awaiting medical discharge.

John 25223563.
Sapper John Booth.
Aged twenty.
9 Parachute Squadron RE.

Injured on 19th July 2008, PB Armagh, Sangin, Helmand Province. Taliban ambush on a vector rescue op. IED blast to rear of Wimik – blown sixty feet into Taliban firing point. QRF on Quadbike taken back to FOB Jackson, Sangin. Medevaced to Camp Bastion, then Queen Elizabeth and Selly Oak.

Broken back four places, broken leg/arm, shattered heel, shrapnel legs, thigh, groin, lung contusion, head injury, ten-week strict bed rest. Told would never walk again, wheelchair-bound, intensive rehab. After treatment returned to front line September 2010 but forced to return after nine months due to previous injuries. Awaiting spinal surgery and rehabilitation.

Frank PO63793G.

Cpl Frank Taylor.

Aged twenty-five.

Special Forces Support Group.

Injured on 1st February 2007 in Helmand Province.

Hit by RPG blast as storming Taliban compound. Casevaced via Black Hawk to Kandahar for initial treatment. Once stabilised flew back to Selly Oak Hospital, Birmingham. After six weeks began recovering physically but mentally struggling. Currently seeing psychologists in an establishment in Berkshire.

Roger 25886967.

Cpl Roger Smith.

Aged thirty-seven.

B Company.

2PWRR.

Injured on 26th August 2008 in Nad Ali, Afghanistan. I was commanding a Snatch three hundred metres short of jab when the vehicle hit an IED. I was blown clear of the vehicle, landing on my right shoulder and neck. Medevaced to Bastion. I had prolapsed discs at C5 and C7 in my upper spine and a dislocated shoulder. Casevaced back to UK. Sent to Selly Oak Hospital. Birmingham where discs at C6 and C7 were replaced. Presently undergoing rehab at Headley Court.

Jean W25031076.
Sgt Jean Barker.
Aged twenty-six.
26 Engineer Regiment 8 Squadron.
Injured on 15th June 2007. I was driving in convoy in the lower Sangin Valley when my Pinzgauer hit an IED. I was thrown from the vehicle, sustaining two broken ankles and a damaged lower back. Medevaced from blast area to Camp Bastion. Flown to UK to Selly Oak Hospital. Sent back to regiment with ongoing physio.
   Awaiting below-knee amputation of right leg and reconstruction of left ankle. Also receiving treatment for PTSD. Discharge date, 11th April 2012.

Darren 25051100.
Bombardier Daz Sobey.
Aged thirty-four.
26th Regiment, Royal Artillery.
Injured on April 2007 on Salisbury Plain whilst commanding 105mm artillery light gun.
   Gun crew accidently crushed me bringing gun into action. Spinal damage and losing use of left arm. Had spinal surgery but remain in chronic pain and reliant on strong medication. Awaiting medical discharge.

Chris 24652173.
Colour Sergeant Chris Ward.
Aged forty-three.
1st Battalion, Royal Green Jackets
Injured in July 2006 by an IED while on patrol in Sangin Valley. Lost both legs, two fingers and both bollocks. Eight weeks at Selly Oak hospital, then fourteen months at Headley Court before voluntary medical discharge. Mentor for the Not Forgotten Association.

Ali 25108692.

Sergeant Ali Briggs.

Aged thirty-six.

1st Battalion, Royal Anglian Regiment.

Injured on 17th June 2008 on Herrick 7 when a mortar round landed in my forward operating base. Shrapnel in my legs, mainly right knee. Casevaced to Bastion where initially treated, then flown back to Selly Oak Hospital, Birmingham. Transferred to Headley Court for intensive rehab. Awaiting elective below-knee amputation.

Simi W1042163.

Lance Cpl Simi Yeats.

Aged thirty-eight.

Injured 16th June 2010 in Hamelm, Germany. Damage to left knee. Realignment of left leg at Frimley Park Hospital. Undergoing physio and rehabilitation at Headley Court, pending Army career outcome.

David 25014876.

Capt David Philips.

Aged thirty-seven.

9 Parachute Squadron, Royal Engineers.

Injured on Herick 8, 2008, Sangin, Afghanistan. Mortar attack. Suffered shrapnel wounds to the stomach and leg. Medevaced to Camp Bastion and transferred to Selly Oak Hospital Birmingham. There for six weeks, three of them in an induced coma. Transferred to Headley Court. Remained for seven months. Suffer from PTSD.

SCENE THREE – JOINING

The soldiers remain in their positions. They begin humming 'Men of Harlech'. Charlie takes a step forward.

Charlie I joined up for a bet. I saw an advert for the Royal Marines – 'Ninety-nine point nine per cent need not apply.' So I applied.

As each soldier speaks they also take a step/wheel forward.

Daniel I was working in Tesco's when I read an article about Sandhurst being short of officers.

Roger Well, the Gulf War had kicked off, hadn't it? Everyone wanted a gun. *I* wanted a gun. My father-in-law had been giving me grief – telling me I couldn't handle it. So I joined. That fucking showed him.

Darren Family tradition. My father was artillery, my uncle's artillery, my great-great-grandfather was artillery. Even my nan was an ack-ack gunner.

Frank When I saw the Twin Towers go down, well, I thought I wanted to be part of it, you know, help sort it out. I was a bricklayer at the time but we'd had a hard couple of winters and we had our son on the way. So yeah, I joined for my family too.

Leroy I can't remember the Twin Towers. I was ten years old when that happened. In my family, though, every male has to serve in the Army. I joined as soon as I could, when I was sixteen. My mother wanted me to wait. She'd already lost two of my brothers. One in the Falklands, another in the Gulf.

Chris I wanted to be a copper, but my dad said coppers don't have no mates, so we went down the careers office and I joined the Army instead. Royal Green Jackets. My old man was dead proud.

Ali His dad was right. Coppers don't have no mates. My grandfather said I'd never amount to anything. When he died I joined up. When I passed out and saw the look on my mum's face I thought great, two birds, one stone. I made my grandad proud and my mum don't think I'm a knobhead any more.

John I just always wanted to. Ever since my older brother gave me this tank you built yourself. I was always running round the woods, that kind of thing. I signed up when I was sixteen. My mum's always supported me. Always.

Jean It was a way out, to be honest. I had an attitude problem. Was either the Army way or the other way, if you know what I mean. The police and my parents pushed me in.

David Every man in my family's served. Crimean War, Boer War, World War One, World War Two. Do you know Psalm 144? It was written in the front of our family bible – 'Blessed be the Lord, my strength, which teaches my hands to war and my fingers to fight.' But it's about security too. For my family. Stability.

The Soldiers remain in their final positions.

SCENE FOUR – RECRUITMENT

Three women enter: Frank's girlfriend Michelle, John's mother Tracy and Charlie's fiancée Lauren.

Michelle He said he was doing it for all of us, our future. And I still believe him. He was. We had our Liam on the way and, well, we needed the money. So yeah, of course I supported him.

Tracy My husband, his step-dad, he was in the Army. So, yeah, I know what it's like. What they're like. And I know he's always wanted to join, from when he was little.

Lauren We met two weeks before he went for his basic training. I was working in a pub. He had to have three shots of tequila before he had the courage to ask me out. He was full of it, even then.

Michelle He really wanted to do something. He wanted to make a difference. And he did, I'm sure of it. There was just so much we didn't know, wasn't there? About what it was going to be like. When he went away. Afterwards.

Tracy But, at the end of the day he's my son, isn't he? He's my baby. I'd never stop him, but, well, it's hard, yeah, it is. Seeing your boy go off like that.

Lauren I could see straight away there was no way he wouldn't go. And I was never going to ask him to choose, was I? I mean, who wants to hear they come second?

A single spotlight upstage discovers Simi. She begins walking downstage, singing a gospel song to the tune of 'His Eyes on the Sparrow'.

Simi
I sing because I'm happy
I sing because I'm free
For his eyes are over all of us
And I know he's watching me.

The other women exit.

When I was seven I had a dream. I was going to live where the Queen lived. And I was going to be a soldier.
I'd seen her when she came to visit on Independence Day. All of us were lining the streets of San Fernando, waving. And she waved back. She had a pink hat, and a matching suit. And as she waved I was shouting, 'I'm going to live where you live! I'm going to live where you live!'
And then I had my dream. I told my mother about it while she was combing my hair.

Young Simi enters and kneels in front of Simi, who begins combing her hair.

Young Simi There were four of us, four girls. My mother kept forgetting our names, so in the mornings when she was getting us ready for school, she numbered us instead, one to four. I was number three.

Beat.

Mummy?

Simi (*as her mother*) Keep your head still, child!

Young Simi I had a dream last night.

Simi (*as her mother*) You always dreaming some stupidness!

Young Simi No, Mum! This is a good one.

Simi (*as her mother*) You always say it's a good one. Go on then. What is it?

Young Simi I dreamt I was a soldier and I lived where the Queen lives.

Simi (*as her mother*) Where the Queen lives? Where the Queen lives? I told you it was a stupid dream! You know where the Queen lives?

Young Simi No.

Beat.

But I can find out.

Simi (*as her mother*) Look, child, get to school before you're late! And stop talking your stupidness!

She ushers Young Simi away.

Young Simi (*to the audience*) Joining the Army wasn't even a thought in my family. I had no father, so Mum was both Mum and Dad. Every time I mentioned my dream she went ballistic.

Simi (*as her mother*) Of course I did! What is to have a girlchild in the Caribbean and be mother, father, everything? You have to keep them close. Where you can see them, reach them.

Young Simi If I was playing in the backyard and went out the gate, she'd come out to pull me back in.

Simi (*as her mother*) You was too far for me to reach out that gate. Too far.

Young Simi But I wanted to do something different. I wanted to go to England. I wanted to be a soldier.
  So one day I woke up and I told her. I was going.

The two women look at each other.

Simi (*as her mother*) Too far. Too far.

Young Simi walks upstage towards a recruiting office.

Young Simi Two weeks after I got to England I saw an advert. 'Be the Best,' it said. 'Join the British Army.' I got on a bus to Edgware, came out of the station and there, in front of me, was a careers centre. So I walked in.

She enters the recruiting office, where Chris sits behind a desk.

Chris Afternoon, how can I help you?

Young Simi I'd like to join the Army.

Chris Well, you've come to the right place. Are you local?

Young Simi Pardon?

Chris Are you from round here?

Young Simi No. I'm from Trinidad. San Fernando. I have my passport.

Chris Right, far enough. Well, let's get started shall we? How old are you?

As Chris asks the question the lights come up on another recruiting office upstage. John and his mother, Tracy, sit across a desk from Roger.

John Sixteen.

Tracy Two months ago, August.

Roger Right, thanks. And was it always the Paras that interested you, John?

John Yeah.

Roger And why's that?

John Well, they're the best, ain't they?

Roger We like to think so. Enjoy your outdoor stuff, do you? Skydiving, water-skiing in Cyprus, scuba diving – (*To Tracy.*) There's some brochures there if you want to take a look – muff diving.

Tracy How long is the training again?

As she asks this the lights come up on another office downstage. Daniel sits across a desk from Frank.

Daniel Thirty-two weeks, if you pass everything first time.

Frank My girlfriend's pregnant. Will I be away for all that time?

Daniel No. There's a break halfway though. Any marriage plans?

Frank We thought we'd wait until I'd finished training.

Daniel Right. Well, yes, that could work. If you pass out on a Friday, you'll be reporting for duty with your new unit on the Monday morning. So there's a couple of days there.

Frank It's that quick?

As he asks the question the lights come up on another office downstage. Leroy sits across a desk from Charlie, who wears his prosthetic leg.

Leroy Can be. A year from now you could be in Afghan. Norway. Belize.

Charlie Sweet.

Leroy And that stuff you hear about women and the uniform? All fucking true. You get your green beret, women all over your cock.

Charlie So when can I get started?

Leroy You can start now if you want to, mate. I'll just get the forms and we'll get cracking.

He wheels away from the desk, revealing he has no legs.

(*As he returns to the desk.*) Everything all right mate?

Charlie Yeah, sorry. It's just. I didn't realise . . . um, well, you've got no legs.

Leroy Well, at least you'll pass the observation test.

Beat.

Look, you're making the right choice, Charlie. When you join the corps you join a family. You'll make friends who'll be closer to you than brothers. Yeah, shit happens, but I wouldn't change any of it. I lost my legs, but I saved my best friend's life that day. You any idea what that feels like? To care that much about something, to care that much about doing your job?

Charlie No.

Leroy Sign here today and you will.

All four recruits – Young Simi, John, Frank and Charlie – sign simultaneously.
Young Simi turns towards the audience.

25

Young Simi I signed up for twenty-two years. Then I got on the bus and went back to my auntie's. When I came in the door I told her, 'Auntie, I'm a soldier.' I was living my dream.

The other recruits also face the audience. They all raise one hand. Young Simi begins the Oath of Allegiance. The others join her in turn until they are all reciting the oath.

I swear by Almighty God that I will be faithful and bear true allegiance to Her Majesty Queen Elizabeth II, her heirs and successors –

Charlie – and that I will as in duty bound honestly and faithfully defend Her Majesty, her heirs and successors –

John – in person, crown and dignity against all enemies –

Frank – and will observe and obey all orders of Her Majesty, her heirs and successors –

All – and of the generals and officers set over me. So help me God.

SCENE FIVE – TRAINING

As the recruits come to the end of the Oath they are joined by John and David. The sound of a train leaving a station. They loiter. Some light cigarettes.
Suddenly Darren marches through them, screaming orders.

Darren Oi! You lot, get fell in! That means get into a fucking line!
Put out that fag, you scraggy little shit! You – stand up straight! Don't you fucking look at me like that, you worthless little shit! Get that fucking hoodie down!

You're in a new gang now! You two, Pinky and Perky, put those fucking phones away!

John Sorry, Sarge.

Darren Sarge? Sarge? Would you like me to massahge your passahge with my sausahge? I'm not your sarge, I'm a bombardier, shitlips!

He turns on the audience.

What you fucking looking at? You! Get a haircut. You! Sit up straight. Don't you fucking smile at me, sonny boy! You think I'm funny, do you? Well, we'll soon see about that.

As Darren marches the recruits around the stage, the Training Song begins.

TRAINING SONG
You will not call me mate,
I am not your friend.
You will not call me sir,
I am not your friend,
You will call me Bombardier,
You will look at me with fear,
For no matter how sweet I may appear,
I am not your friend!

When I say 'Sit up', you do. (Yes, we do!)
When I say 'Brace up', you do. (Yes, we do!)
When I say 'Stand to', stand to. (Yes, we do!)
You will never ask me why.
And when I say 'Jump!',
You will ask 'How high?'

Polish boots is what you do. (Yes, we do!)
You love starch and Brasso too. (Yes, we do!)
Thinking you can leave to me.
Uniform is your ID.
In your sleep, you'll dream PT. (Yes, we do!)

27

Just one way to survive:
You all work as a team.
To make it out alive,
You all work as a team.
Close as twins inside the womb,
Close as corpses in a tomb,
Like a bride astride a groom,
You all work as a team.

Feel the burn, enjoy the pain. (Feel the burn!)
Pain is pleasure, tell your brain. (Feel the burn!)
You're alive, so pain is gain! (Feel the burn!)
Feeling pain you won't succumb,
And you won't feel fear till you're feeling numb.

Clean your rifle, then yourself. (My weapon, myself!)
Think of rifle, then yourself. (My weapon, myself!)
When your rifle's really clean,
And by clean I mean pristine,
You can load your magazine.
(My weapon, myself!)
(My weapon, myself!) (My weapon, myself!)
(My weapon, myself!)(My weapon, myself!)
(My weapon, myself!)(My weapon, myself!)
(My weapon, myself!)

Darren Squad will move to the right in file, right turn!
By fronts, quick march! Left right left right . . .

The recruits are marched offstage.

SCENE SIX – BRIEFING I

Daniel enters with a white screen. A map of Afghanistan is projected on to it. He addresses the audience as if at a military briefing.

Daniel Thank you, Sergeant Barker. British forces first

entered Afghanistan in 1839. This first Afghan War resulted in a British withdrawal.

The Second Afghan War was fought in 1878, again resulting in a British withdrawal.

We entered Afghanistan for a third time in 1919 and withdrew the same year, celebrated annually on Afghan Independence Day on 19th August. These three Afghan wars are sometimes referred to as 'The Great Game'.

A communist-backed coup precipitated an invasion by the Soviet Union in 1979. This invasion was resisted by the Mujahaddin, resulting in Soviet withdrawal ten years later in '89.

Between '92 and 2001 the Taliban gained control of the country. They imposed strict Shari'a law and provided a safe haven for Al Qa'eda.

The Taliban were overthrown by the Northern Alliance and US/UK forces in 2001. They still remain active in southern parts of the country including Helmand Province, where British forces have had locations in Sangin, Kajaki, Musa Qala, Nad Ali, Gereshk, Lashkar Gah, Garmsir and many more.

Helmand Province covers a total area of 59,000 square kilometres, larger than Wales and Northern Ireland put together. In 2002 the British had three hundred troops on the ground. In 2005 we had three thousand, in 2012 nine thousand, five hundred. We currently have around six thousand servicemen and women in the country.

Afghanistan has always been a strategic crossroads for the region, and in today's operating environment its neighbours Pakistan and Iran both have significant interests in the country. Some of the players have changed, but the playing field remains the same.

The Great Game, ladies and gentleman, continues.

Daniel exits.

SCENE SEVEN – FIELD MEDIC COURSE

The call to evening prayer from a minaret. 'Chasing Cars' by Snow Patrol plays faintly in the background.
David and Roger march in with John, who wears full combat uniform, Osprey, helmet.

David Right, forget what you learnt on your FA1s, BCTD, CFX or whatever. For the next six months this is the only course you need to remember. If you listen up it'll either save your life or one of your oppos, so listen up good. John! Now, John here has kindly agreed to be our puppet today. Say hello, John.

John Hello, John.

David As you can see John's all kitted out to take on the Tali. Helmet, Osprey, weapon system. Combined weight of 70 to 80 kilos. It's hot today, isn't it? Well, get used to it, because it's always fucking hot. Except when it's cold, and then it's fucking cold. Either way, whatever the weather, you're going to be spending a lot of your time out here carrying this load.

Roger points to a member of the audience.

Roger Want to know what that feels like?

He points at another person in the audience.

Like having him on your back. All day. But however tired you might get, you do not reduce your kit. Why? Because everything you need to protect yourself, to survive or to save your mucka, is carried here, on your person.

Roger begins going through John's pouches and pockets, pulling out the kit.

Ammunition, bayonet, pistol, PRR, morphine – lose that and you will be in a world of pain! Field dressings, compression bandages. Celox gauze – remember every hole's a goal! Ashman's seal for those sucking chest wounds. Tourniquet! High and tight! Tight is right! And always check the back of the fucking wound too!

David So much for the kit. Now let's get to the stuff that really matters. (*To John.*) Strip down, John.

John hesitates.

Roger You heard him. Down to your blast pants.

As John removes his uniform.

David Kit changes. Always has, always will. But human anatomy doesn't change. And that's why you'd better listen up good because this could make the difference between your mate going home on a stretcher or in a body bag.

He takes out a red marker pen. As he talks he draws on John's body.

Let's start with the basics, shall we?

He holds up the bottle of water.

This is a litre of water. John's got five litres of blood in his body. He can lose a litre of that, no problem. Two litres, getting tricky. More than that, he should start to worry. His heart, about the size of a fist, is here. When he starts oozing, this is pumping the juice from his arteries. Going south through his thoracic aorta, out here, along his arms, and down here, along his thighs. And up here, supplying his tiny mind, his carotid artery. Right, so things have gone wrong for John and he's stepped on an IED.

What injuries is he likely to sustain? Probably lose a leg, if he's lucky amputated here, or unlucky, here. So that's gone, off in someone else's compound. What else? He'll be fragged here on his face, and here along the side of his neck. It's a conical blast wave, remember, so here under his arms too. Some big chunks out of his legs from the stones and crap on the ground. Probably a chunk out of the arm, here. Fragged along side of the chest.

Where's his weapon gone? That's right, straight up into his grid. Broken jaw, fractured zygoma, bit of blast ear. Pressure injury to the lungs. Probably lose a few fingers too. What else are we forgetting? What's here, biggest bone in the body? That's right, his femur. Where's that going? Smash, into his pelvis. Serious injury? You bet! Dislocated shoulder.

If he isn't wearing his shades, sand, dirt and stones in his eyes.

He points to John's genitals.

What's going to happen to this bad boy? If he's wearing his blast pants, hopefully nothing. If he's not? The eyelets from his boots are going to fly up, penetrate his nut sack, sever his penis. It's one of the first questions they'll ask you. 'Have I got my cock and balls?' If he's not wearing blast pants, you can tell him yes, but he'll be pissing in six different directions for the rest of his life. Probably lost both arse cheeks too. So, respect the men whose injuries we've learnt from, and wear those fucking pants!

Right, that's enough of you, John.

John takes a white towel and walks downstage, cleaning the marker pen from his body, turning the towel red.

Roger Bullet wounds! You're out on patrol and the tree line's opened up on you, like it does. Your mate's gone down, small entry wound on the front, big exit wound in the back. You've got to pack that exit wound while still laying down rounds in the opposite direction. So what you going to do?

Roger's voice fades away as the spot tightens to isolate John.

John He's right, you know. Some things don't change. Weapons change. Battlefields change. Wars change. But there's one thing that's never changed.

He pats his own chest.

This. Fight with stones. Fight with swords. Fight with missiles. This is where the fight happens. This is where the speeches end. The resolutions. This is where victory or defeat happens. The politics. This is where war happens. Here. On the bodies of men. Boys. We try and take theirs apart. They try and take ours apart. It's as simple as that.

He turns and walks upstage. The lights come up to reveal a FOB – temporary showers and toilets, sandbags, Hesco blocks. The heads of Ali and Roger can be seen above a screen in front of the toilets. Ali ducks below the screen. The sound of him vomiting. He reappears.

SCENE EIGHT – COMMS

Darren enters with a sack of mail.

Darren Mail's here, lads.

Ali Ah, at last! About fucking time too!

Other Soldiers begin to gather around Darren as he hands out the mail. Charlie and Chris wear their prosthetics so appears to have both legs intact.

Darren Ward . . . Smith . . . Philips . . . Briggs . . .

Ali Get mine for me will you, mate?

Darren Taylor . . . Sir . . . Barker . . .

As each soldier receives their bluey or package they drift to a more private place.

Barker . . . Barker . . . and Barker.

Jean is given a pile of packages.

Charlie You're crated, Barker. So crated.

Darren Yeats . . . Booth . . . Fowler . . .

As the Soldiers open their bluies, the Letter Writers appear.

Lauren Charlie, I miss you so much –

Michelle Hey babe! I hope you get this soon . . . never soon enough though, is it?

Tracy Dear son, a few more parcels for you. No chocolate this time, like you asked. But lots of Haribo and shower gel!

The Soldiers continue to read their bluies as the female Letter Writers sing:

Letter Writers (*sung*)
Hope you get this, hope you're safe, hope everything's all right. Miss you.
Everyone here is thinking of you, we've heard nothing on the news. Miss you.
Look after yourself, my love, and come home soon.

Chris When you're in the FOBs most of the time bluies is all you get. Only once, maybe twice every two months. There's one I'll always remember. My daughter drew me a birthday cake. And my son, he's got special needs see, but he managed to write his name. It might not sound like much, but I was crying. It chokes you up, it does.

John You have to take yourself away, somewhere quiet. It makes you miss home, miss everyone there. You realise how long it'll be before you see them again.

34

Simi For three months I didn't get any bluies. It took so long from Trinidad to England to Iraq. Every time the mail came, I'd just be waiting, feeling alone. The boys on camp even started writing to me, just so I'd have some mail! But then one day I saw a Trinidad and Tobago stamp. I couldn't believe it. I almost screamed down the whole of the RHQ. Seeing their names, Mummy's handwriting. I rub it all over my face, so it would stay with me. I even slept with it! Every time I turned over, I'd reach under my pillow to check it was there. Because it was a lifeline, that bluey. It really was. A lifeline home.

The Soldiers begin to write. As their recipients open their letters the Soldiers sing.

Soldiers (*sung*)
Please don't worry, I'm with a good bunch of lads.
And, you know, we look out for each other.

Send my love to Mum and Dad.
I don't know when I'll call again.

All my love, all my love.

Tracy I saw Mr Roberts yesterday. Your old Geography teacher? He said everyone at school is so proud of you.

Leroy Alright, Big Rog! Chris here. Bet you weren't expecting this. Send my best to the lads and let them know I'm doing fine – there are more nurses here at the QE than I know what to do with!

Michelle PS. Sent you a special treat – just so you don't forget what's waiting for you back home. But keep this one to yourself!

Roger Leroy mate! All the lads say you're a jack bastard for pissing off early. Jonesy reckons you knew it was there but stepped on it anyway so you could dodge the rest of the tour. Mind you, can't blame you – those QE Nurses sound worth it!

Frank You mustn't worry about me, baby, I'll be fine. But I am missing you loads. I think my balls are going to explode!

Leroy Hearing from the lads after I got back helped loads. Yeah, those bluies meant a lot.

Lauren He asked me to send him porn, which I did. But I never sent him photos of *me* like that. I've seen too many of the ones sent by the other girls to fall for that. I mean, I'm not going to provide relief for the whole unit!

Chris I'm losing lots of weight in this heat. You'll have a new man when I come home!

Charlie I head out on a 'camping trip' with the 'boy scouts' next week. I'll call as soon as I can, I promise!

Soldiers (*sung*)
 Please don't worry, I'm with a good bunch of lads.
 And, you know, we look out for each other.

Letter Writers (*sung*)
 Hope you get this, hope you're safe, hope everything's
 all right. Miss you.

Soldiers (*sung*)
 Send my love to Mum and Dad.
 I don't know when I'll call again.

Letter Writers (*sung*)
 Everyone here is thinking of you.
 We've heard nothing on the news. Miss you.

Soldiers (*sung*)
 All my love, all my love.

Letter Writers (*sung*)
 Look after yourself, my love. And come home soon.

Daniel No one gets to keep their mobile phone. They're too easy to intercept. Or if the enemy get hold of the sim card, then they phone the families at home, tell them their son or daughter has been captured. Which isn't good. So each week we get twenty welfare minutes on the sat phone instead. It's great, to hear your wife's voice, to speak to the kids. But it's really hard too. You *feel* the distance. After speaking with them I have to try really hard to disconnect from them again. And saying goodbye, that's the hardest. Saying goodbye.

Letter Writers (*sung*)
Kiss, kiss. Love you. Kiss, kiss. Love you.
PS. PS. Love you. Love you.

Soldiers (*sung*)
All my love. All my love. All my love.

Letter Writers (*sung*)
Kiss, kiss. Love you. Kiss, kiss. Love you.

The singing repeats and fades as both groups return to reading their letters on either side of the stage. Roger is watching John, who looks distressed.

Roger Of course sometimes the news from home is bad news. There's always a few Dear Johns. But you can't have one of your boys out on patrol who hasn't got his head on the job. So you've got to sort them out, whatever it takes.

Chris Oi, Booth. What you got there?

Frank She hasn't, has she? The bitch.

John Yeah, she has.

Chris Come on then.

Chris takes the letter from John.

'Dear John' – Fuck, I can't believe she actually gets to write that. 'Dear John, I know this will be hard for you to read, but please believe me this is even harder for me to say.'

Darren Yeah, I bet it is, love, cos you've got mortars coming in and only ration packs for the next five months too, haven't you?

Chris 'I'm just not sure I can do this any more.'

Ali More like she's doing some other bloke down the pub.

Chris 'When I read about that soldier killed last week, I felt so sick, thinking it could have been you.'

Frank So you thought you'd bin him. Yeah, nice.

Chris 'I know I said I would wait for you, but I didn't know it would be like this.'

Chris hands the bluey back to John. The Soldiers start singing 'Achy Breaky Heart'.
 John cracks a smile.
 All exit except for Roger.

Roger You've got to defuse stuff quickly, and humour's the best way to do that. Attack, like they say, it's the best form of defence, isn't it?

Lights come up on Sarah, Daniel's wife. She is dressed in funeral black, her head bowed.

Chaplain (*voice-over*) We are gathered here today to honour the life and memory of Lance Corporal Andrew Jones, a young man of extraordinary courage who was willing to lay down his life for the lives of others and to pay the ultimate sacrifice in the defence of his country.

Offstage the Soldiers begin singing 'Abide with Me'. The hymn continues under the following action.
 Sarah walks downstage.

Sarah It's wonderful when he calls, of course it is. What wife doesn't want to hear from their husband? To know he's safe . . . But it's so frustrating too. I have to talk to

him about all this ordinary stuff, when all I really want
to ask him is, were you shot at today? Are you OK? Are
you going out on any more ops? But I can't, can I?
Because he can't tell me. Because all I'll get is silence.
And I understand that, I do. Because sometimes there are
things I can't tell him either.

*A phone rings. Sarah answers. The lights come up on
the other side of the stage to reveal Daniel on a sat
phone. Frank waits a little way behind him.*

Daniel Darling? Darling, it's me.

Sarah Oh, it's so good to hear you. How are you?

Daniel I'm fine, fine.

Sarah Did you get the recipes?

Daniel Yes, I did. Thanks. Though not sure I'm really
doing them justice.

Beat.

Sarah How is it out there?

Daniel Hot. Even hotter than before, if that's possible.

Sarah Right.

Daniel And there?

Sarah All fine. Good. Been raining today. Lucy's at
netball though, so . . .

Daniel Oh yes. Yes, that's Tuesdays and Thursdays now,
isn't it?

Sarah Yes. She sent you a bluey yesterday.

Daniel Great. Did she get mine?

Sarah Not yet, no.

Beat.

Daniel Did you hear about Jones?

Sarah Yes, I did. His poor mother. I've written to her.

Daniel Yes, so have I.

Beat.

But you mustn't worry. Everything's fine, really.

Sarah Right. Yes.

The phone starts beeping.

Daniel Look, darling, I think I'm about to run out of minutes. I'm so sorry. I'll top up tomorrow.

Sarah OK. Don't forget we'll be at your mother's next week.

Daniel Yes. Of course. I love you.

Sarah I love you too.

The line goes dead. They both look at their handsets for a moment. Daniel hands the sat phone to Frank. As Frank dials, Daniel walks downstage.
Just before he speaks we see Michelle take Sarah's place to answer Frank's call. She carries a baby with one hand, holds the phone in her other. We don't hear their conversation.

Daniel Sometimes I think we say more with our silences than we do with our words. But it has to be that way. And not just for security. If she knew what I was doing, well, it would be hell for her. But I understand it must be just as difficult not knowing. But what can we do? It's still worth it – hearing her voice, speaking to Lucy. It's about staying in touch, isn't it? About staying in contact.

As soon as Daniel says the word 'contact' –

All Soldiers (*shouted*) CONTACT!

The sound of small arms fire, mortars, UGLs and RPGs.

The Soldiers scramble for helmets and weapons and begin laying down rounds in a defensive shoot.

Frank tries to turn off the sat phone, but fails. Michelle is left listening to the contact. She shouts Frank's name into the phone but her voice is drowned by the gunfire.

The sound of battle stops and a single spot lights Michelle.

Michelle I had to listen to that contact for over five minutes. Explosions. Bullets. Shouting. It was two weeks before I heard from him again.

Fade to black.

SCENE NINE – CONTACT

Charlie sits opposite a Psychologist. As they talk, the silhouette of a man with a Vallon man occasionally passes them.

Charlie What's it like? Jeez, well, kinda like everything you imagine. And not. I mean, when I first got out there it was like I was watching *Apocalypse Now*. I didn't know where to look, where to go, what was dangerous, what was safe. You come off the Chinook and the heat hits you like a punch in the face. And the smell. Shit and dust. It was the first time I'd heard a proper weapons system, outside the firing range. And, I mean, it's being discharged *at* you. Crack – thump. Crack – thump. The crack of the bullet snapping the air, *then* the thump of the weapon.

Psychologist And what about your first contact? How did you find that?

Charlie Well, it kinda found us really. They attacked our compound and, I won't lie, Doc, it was fucking great. It was like, finally, we get to do our job. We'd had weeks of just gash sweeps, sangar duty, that kinda shit. So to finally have a defensive shoot – it was the best day of my military career. It was simple, you know? They brought the fight to us. We won, they lost. We suffered no casualties, but lots of our guys got confirmed kills. So yeah, it felt really, really good.

The following speeches are projected on to the stage.

Roger You can't tell how you'll react. When that first RPG went across our bonnet me and Jimmy just looked at each other, then started laughing. A month later he was dead, killed by one.

Frank Your training kicks in. There's so much adrenalin the body takes over. And you've got rounds coming the other way too, at you, so yeah, I was just trying to stay alive.

Simi It was the kids that were my deepest surprise. On Telic 8. Coming at you with automatic weapons, petrol bombs. Eleven, twelve years old. And you have to make that choice. It's you or them. You fire some rounds over their heads, and you hope they run away. But if they don't, then . . .

Richard I loved my first contact. I was in an orchard with my mate Parry. A sniper's round just missed my head. I felt it brush past my face. We didn't have our gats, so we ran for it, back to the camp, with the whole orchard being thrown up around us. And Parry, he starts singing from behind me, 'Run rabbit, run rabbit, run, run, run.' Just over and over.

Roger, Frank and John enter as a patrol in full combat gear. They move very slowly in formation downstage. Daniel's speech is also projected.

Daniel On patrol you've got your eyes down all the time, trying to follow the Vallon man's route exactly

Then the next day we'd be at a Shura, a gathering of the local elders. And for all I knew the hand I was shaking had planted the bomb that blew up one of my boys the week before.

Psychologist And how did that experience change you? Over the tours?

Charlie Well the war changed, didn't it? Afghanistan changed. I mean, on Herrick 5 it was Wild West stuff, bandit country. Ten-dollar Taliban doing Beirut unloads. A lot of spray and pray, shoot and scoot. But by Herrick 14 it was proper guerilla warfare. I mean, Sangin was IED central. Low metal content, infra-red switches, strapping bombs to donkeys. They were even planting decoys so they could watch how we examined them. You had to respect your enemy. I mean, the guy who did this to me did a really, really good job. It was a legacy IED, laid a while ago. But the batteries – those batteries had been changed regularly, to keep it active.

Psychologist Were you out on patrol often?

Charlie Yeah. I mean, you've got to take the fight to them, haven't you? You can't just sit back in the compound with your thumb firmly up your ass. But I'll tell you, Doc, that first time I stepped outside the gate, my mouth went dry. I had to take a sip from my CamelBak straight away because . . . well, we were suddenly outside our comfort zone. You *know* that once you're out that gate anything could happen, at any time. And that it probably will. Every day we were playing Afghan roulette.

Roger We'd snake, spread out, change our routes. We had two Vallon men on most patrols, and ECMs. But sometimes there was nothing you could do. There were some bad days. But there were good days too, you know, when you're seeing them drop.

Frank We'd always be watching the atmospherics. If you see the women and children start to leave, or some bloke who might be dicking you, we'd go firm, straight away. Take no chances.

John On my second tour we never saw them, not once. It was like fighting ghosts. When we did night ops sometimes they'd communicate by howling like animals, like dogs. That could be pretty scary. I took a Pashtun language course before I went out. That helped loads. I could talk to people when we were out on patrol. Sometimes they'd tell us where the Taliban were, or warn us off certain routes.

Psychologist And what about relations with the locals? Did you have much interaction?

Charlie Well, yeah, sure, hearts and minds and all that. But that was the biggest change of all, Doc. I mean, knowing *who* the enemy were. On the early tours you could bet anyone still in the smashed-up village you were occupying was up to no good. But then later? On Herrick 12, 13, 14? It was a whole different ball game. Farmers, bazaars, kids, families. So the war card changed, didn't it? You had to PID someone before you fired.

Psychologist PID?

Charlie Positively identify. Which I completely understand, but it was like we were stuck between these two fucking TLAs – PID and IED with old bootneck getting fucked over in the middle.

Beat.

The only way I can explain it is that you're not living with 'if' any more, but 'when'. A company loses a man and things change. You're fighting for the man next to you. Fuck anything else. But at the same time you're waking up every day expecting something to happen. It's

44

like there's five of you in a car, going on a road trip, but you *know* at the end of that trip two of you will have lost your legs, one of you will be dead and another one will be wounded. You just don't know who, or when.

Psychologist Do you want to talk about your 'when', Charlie?

Beat.

Charlie Sure. I was taking part in an op . . .

Simi enters. She begins singing her gospel song to the tune of 'His Eyes on the Sparrow'.

Daniel I was commanding a company . . .

John I was on top cover . . .

Frank I was against a wall . . .

Roger I was in a Snatch . . .

Young Simi I was in the comms room . . .

Chris I was on patrol . . .

All When / When / When / When . . .

A sudden simultaneous moment of contact. The sound of explosions and gunfire. In slow motion Frank is hit by an RPG. John is blown from his vehicle. Roger's Snatch turns over. Chris, Daniel, Charlie and Leroy are hit by IEDs. Simi, still singing, has joined Young Simi in the centre of the stage.

Young Simi There were two mortars, back to back. The first one killed my best friend. I was trying to get to him when the second one brought the wall down on me.

She kneels in front of Simi.

I was trapped. They were trying to dig me out. But all I could hear was Mummy, singing the song we always sang.

As Young Simi also starts singing 'His Eyes on the Sparrow', Simi combs her hair, as in the earlier scene. All around them the moments of wounding continue.
The non-wounded Soldiers become medics. Shouts of 'Man Down!', 'Morphine!', T1 casualty reports.
John is crouched over Chris, Darren over Daniel.
As the medics work the wounded Soldiers sit up to speak.

Daniel I was blown twenty metres . . .

Frank I heard the rocket coming in . . .

John I was blown sixty feet . . .

Chris I caught the full force . . .

Roger The Snatch went over and I hit the roof . . .

Daniel The shrapnel went through the back of my brain . . .

Frank It shattered my cheek bone, pierced my eye . . .

John My mates thought I'd bought it, that I was pink mist . . .

Chris I felt the sand hitting my face . . .

Roger I could hear the others screaming, as it filled with water . . .

Simi and Young Simi's singing fades to silence.

John And then there was silence . . .

Frank Just this ringing in my ears, nothing else . . .

Chris Just a blue sky above me . . .

Daniel And nothing else . . .

All lie down to be treated again. Leroy sits up on the other side of the stage.

46

Leroy My mate had been shot. So I was like, fuck this! Osprey off, helmet off, dropped my GPMG. Got him over my shoulder and ran for it. Then, everything went dark. No boom, no hitting the ground, no pain. I was just lying on the floor.

He lies back down as John and Roger run over to him.

John Fuck! You all right, mate?

Leroy Yeah, yeah, I'm good.

Roger Yeah, you fucking look it, mate.

Leroy What's that supposed to mean?

Roger and John start treating him.

John You're going to be OK, mate, you're going to be OK.

Leroy looks up and sees his legs have gone.

Leroy Fuck! Oh fuck!

Roger You've been hit by an IED, mate. But you're going to be fine, you're going to be fine.

John checks his balls.

You've still got your balls, mate.

Leroy Fuck, I'm going to die! I'm going to die! Give me a cigarette! Give me a cigarette!

Roger You're not going to die.

John We can't give you a fag, we can't, mate.

Leroy I'm going to fucking die, give me what I want!

John hands him a fag, and lights it. John, Roger and Leroy all inhale deeply.

I swear, that fag went down in one drag. My right leg was still hanging by a thread but as they carried me away it fell off and rolled into a ditch. I was like, 'Get my leg, get my fucking leg.' They couldn't reach it, so the lads gave me a stick, said 'Here's your fucking leg,' and at the time I could have sworn it was. The last thing I remember is passing out in the chopper, thinking, 'Fuck me, I didn't even have any last words.' Apparently I came round again in Bastion. I was crying, screaming for my mum. But I don't remember any of that.

As Roger and John exit carrying Leroy –
Sarah and Lauren enter to stand in front of two
screened hospital beds.

Sarah For three weeks we experienced two different kinds of hell. He was suffering hallucinations in his coma, while I was out here, not knowing if he was going to live or die. It was strange, because he looked perfect. He was dirty, but he was tanned too, and really lean and fit. And his skin . . . they all come back with such good skin. Sand-blasted, smooth. But he wasn't perfect. Far from it.

Beat.

On the first night, just after he was brought in, I went to have a cup of tea in the waiting room. There were two other women in there, on their knees, on the floor, praying. They were wearing burkas. I know I shouldn't have, but I felt so angry at them. I mean, Daniel was fighting for his life next door. But then I heard them say his name. Major Daniel Thomas. And I realised they were praying for him. They were praying for all the patients on the ward.

Lauren paces up and down.

Lauren Please save him. Please, oh please. I promise if you do I'll come to church every week. I will. I'll go and see Mum more often. I'll cut back on the drink. I'll . . .

I'll stop smoking. Really. I will. Just let him live. Please let him live.

A Nurse enters.

Nurse Miss Preston?

Lauren Yes. That's me.

Nurse You're Charles's . . .

Lauren Fiancée. Yes, yes, I am. Is he OK? Is he going to be all right?

Nurse Well, he's been really put through it. But yes. He's going to pull through.

She flings her arms around him.

Lauren Oh God, thank you! Thank you so much! Can I see him?

Nurse Not yet. He's still in surgery. But in about an hour or so, that should be fine.

The Nurse exits. Lauren roots in her bag for a cigarette.

Lauren Oh thank you, thank you!

She pulls out a cigarette and is about to light it when she pauses. She looks up.

After this. OK? I promise. Last one.

The lights fade up on Charlie and the Psychologist upstage.

Charlie But like I said, I don't remember any of that. I was there, but I wasn't.

Psychologist Right.

The faint sound of military radio chatter, the thudding of a helicopter, building through his speech.

Charlie I don't remember waking up.

49

I don't remember eating breakfast.

I don't remember being given orders, or loading up, or leaving the compound.

I don't remember going where we went.

I don't remember walking through an archway, a low archway.

I don't remember the IED going off.

None of that.

Beat.

Just that taste. Grit in the mouth. And a few sounds, I guess. I remember a few sounds.

The sounds begin to fade.

But that's because it's the last to go, I guess. Your hearing. Your hearing's the last to go.

The sounds fade to silence.

Fade to black.

Act Two

SCENE ONE – PHYSIO

Physio room.
  Classical music.
  Lights come up to reveal an amputee wearing a regimental T-shirt sitting on a therapeutic ball working with his physiotherapist. Using a pair of bats, they hit a bright orange balloon back and forth. Other patients enter, all wearing regimental T-shirts. Other physios also enter. They begin performing different exercises.
  Charlie enters on crutches.

Charlie Welcome back. So, yeah, this is where we come afterwards. When we survive. Personally I thought I was going to Heaven. I'm not kidding, a lot of us here did. You're floating on the morphine, you're being casevaced into the heelo. There's this ringing in your ears and a blue sky above you. You've just been blown up – where do you think *you'd* be going?

Turns out I was wrong though. Wasn't Heaven. It was Selly Oak. Then here.

  Beat.

It's a bit like doing basic training again – 'Break to build', that's what they told us back then. Well, we're sure as hell broken now, aren't we? So, plenty of building to be done. Learning drills and skills for our 'new normal'. Our new world. Our 'brave new world'. That has such creatures in it . . .

So yeah, this is, I guess, our new drill square. The physios our new PT instructors. The doctors, consultants, our majors and generals. Prosthetics, wheelchairs, meds, our new kit. The operations our, well, new operations. It's a bit of a freak show to be honest with you. I wasn't too happy about it at first, I mean, a few weeks ago I was a steely-eyed dealer of death. Then, wham, bam, thank you mam, and I'm in this circus. Seals on bouncy balls. In Surrey.

He looks about the arches of the set.

And very nice it is too. Big grounds, gardens, orchards, regular Downton fucking Abbey.

As Charlie takes his place in the physio room Simi enters, wearing headphones. Her physio tells her to remove them.
As she does the music switches from classical to dance. The exercises begin to syncopate into a choreographed dance.

SCENE TWO — FLASHBACK

The physio dance routine is just starting to build when it is interrupted by a massive blast. A cloud of dust blows in from offstage. All the patients and physios collapse to the floor. The stage darkens. Torch beams sweep the scene as two soldiers in full combat gear, Frank and Darren, enter from the direction of the blast. They are panicked by what they see.

Darren Oh Jesus. Fuck, fuck! They're locals!

Frank They said it was empty!

Darren Well, it obviously fucking wasn't, was it?

Darren begins checking for signs of life.

Frank But we saw them leaving! We saw them fucking leaving!

Daniel enters.

Daniel Jesus Christ! What the fuck is this, Sobey?

Darren We didn't know, sir!

Daniel Any survivors?

Darren No sir.

Frank We saw them leave! We saw them fucking leaving!

Daniel Zero two zero alpha. Contact. Civilian casualties. Wait out. Move on through. Sobey? Clear?

Darren moves to check their exit.

Darren Clear.

Daniel Taylor. For fuck's sake, Taylor!

Frank and Darren exit. Daniel remains, looking at the bodies about him. A faint musical score begins towards the end of his speech.

OPTAG prepares you for most things. But there's no training for this. Seeing it, smelling it. Which is why when some of us come back from Afghan, Afghan stays with us. Or us with it. You walk these corridors at night and, believe me, you'll hear a bit of Afghan behind every door. Sangin . . . Kajaki . . .

He begins to move upstage left, picking his way through the bodies.

Musa Qala . . . Nad Ali . . . Gereshk . . . Lashkar Gah . . . Garmsir . . . FOB Gibraltar . . . FOB Jackson . . . FOB Inkerman . . .

SCENE THREE – SLEEP

Daniel exits. The bodies remain motionless for a moment before beginning to shift and turn. As the musical score gets louder they become syncopated, repeating a sequence of movements of discomfort.

Women

It's not re-living it. It's living it. You're in it. You're there, doing it.

All

Worse at night, always worse at night. Worse at night, always worse at night.

Men

Scared. Scared to close my eyes. Scared to put my head on the pillow.

Scared. Scared to close my eyes. Scared to put my head on the pillow.

All

It's not re-living it. It's living it. You're in it. You're there, doing it.

Worse at night, always worse at night. Worse at night, always worse at night.

John For two years I couldn't sleep. Every fucking night. Just images, flicking through. Being blown up. Prodding through dead bodies in some fucking IED factory. Just all sorts of crazy shit, flicking, bouncing from one to the other. I'd be banging my head against the wall, just to take my mind off it, then . . . then I'm like, yeah, that fucking hurts.

David (*solo*) It's not re-living it. It's living it. You're in it. You're there, doing it.

All

Worse at night, always worse at night. Worse at night, always worse at night.

Roger I had to stay up. I forced myself not to go to sleep. As soon as you close your eyes you see them again. All sorts of situations. Rounds going past your head. Bodies of kids floating downstream. And you think to yourself, why am I fucking here? Why aren't I dead?

Angus Scared, scared to close my eyes. Scared to put my head on the pillow.

Women
   It's not re-living it, it's living it. You're in it, you're there, doing it.

Leroy Mine has its own timetable. It'll come and go. It's like, really awkward. It's space that brings it on. If I sleep in a double bed, then I dream I'm on patrol again. But in my sleep I can control where we go. I still get blown up, though. Every time. Sometimes I'm in my wheelchair, but no one says anything, like, 'Why's Leroy in a fucking wheelchair?' But, yeah, if I sleep in a corner, up against a wall, holding my stumps, that makes it go away.

Charlie For my missus I'm the nightmare. Sweating, reaching for my weapon, taking cover across the carpet. She has to sleep in the corner of the bed. Or I just stay awake. Sometimes I hit myself in the face. To take my mind off it. Or you drink. Hopefully between finishing drinking and falling asleep you don't have too much time to think. Hopefully.

Richard If you do you're fucked –

Chris Fucked –

Roger Fucked –

All Fucked.

Lauren He was drinking so much he'd just collapse into bed and then, God! The snoring! All night.

Michelle He thrashes around. And the sweating. The sweating's the worst. One night he was shouting, 'Contact!' 'Contact!' So I touched him, to wake him, and . . . and he punched me in the face.

Sarah For months he didn't sleep. He doesn't like the silence, it gives him time to think. I have it too. It was five in the morning when they came to tell me. And now I wake every morning at five. That knock on the door, it's in my head, in my body clock, forever.

Women
It's not re-living it, it's living it. You're in it, you're there, doing it.

All
Worse at night, always worse at night. Worse at night, always worse at night.

Men
Scared, scared to close my eyes. Scared to put my head on the pillow.
Scared, scared to close my eyes. Scared to put my head on the pillow.

Women
It's not re-living it, it's living it. You're in it, you're there, doing it.

All
Worse at night, always worse at night. Worse at night, always worse at night.

John It's the pain that triggers it. It's always there, bubbling away, but worse at night. Always worse at night.

Chris Sometimes I just cry, because of the pain, the things it makes me think about.

Leroy It won't go away. It makes me want to smash something. I can't do anything to stop it. Like nails under the skin.

Roger It's all down the left side of my neck, in my brain, down my shoulder and into my back. I try to put it in on a shelf, over there. I use distractions too – reading poetry, stripping my weapons, a shitload of drugs. But then sometimes it just takes over and that's when I have to ring the kids' mum and say, 'I can't have them this weekend.' And that's terrible, because it's my kids that keep me going.

All exit.

SCENE FOUR – BRIEFING 2

Daniel enters upstage in his major's uniform. He begins to walk downstage.

Daniel Nostalgia.
  Melancholia.
  Wind contusions.
  Soldier's heart.
  Abreaction.
  Effort syndrome.
  NYDM (not yet diagnosed – mental).
  NYDN (not yet diagnosed – nervous).
  Exhaustion.
  Battle exhaustion.
  Combat exhaustion.
  Shell shock.
  Neurasthenia.
  Traumatic neurosis.
  Psycho neurosis.
  Fear neurosis.
  Battle neurosis.
  Lack of moral fibre.
  Old sergeant syndrome.
  War syndrome.
  Combat fatigue.
  Acute stress disorder.

Acute stress reaction.
Combat stress reaction.
Post-combat disorder.
Post-war disorder.
Post-traumatic illness.
Post-traumatic disorder.
Post-traumatic stress disorder.

Daniel exits.

SCENE FIVE – COMMON ROOM

The common room of a PRU. A group of wounded and injured soldiers congregates around a singing teacher who leads them in 'The Grand Old Duke of York'.

All
The grand old Duke of York,
He had ten thousand men.
He marched them up to the top of the hill,
And he marched them down again.
And when they were up they were up,
And when they were down they were down,
And when they were only halfway up,
They were neither up nor down.

Singing Teacher No, no, no. Stop, stop. Enunciate, enunciate. The Grand Old Duke of York!

Leroy (*wheeling away*) This is bollocks.

Singing Teacher Leroy. Leroy, where are you going?

Leroy For a fag.

He exits.
Others begin to drift away.

Singing Teacher Right, OK. Yes, OK, let's take a break. Fifteen minutes. Back here at two!

The Soldiers disperse. Chris is on his laptop. The others sit in a group.

Ali Who does he think we are? The Army Wives' Choir?

Frank Ah come on! It's for BLESMA. You have that leg off and the cash we raise'll be going straight to you.

Ali Well, we'd better come up with something better than 'Grand Old Duke of York' then, hadn't we? Cos last time I checked a top-of-the-range C-leg cost more than fucking 50p.

Frank inserts a DVD into his laptop and starts working.

Roger Sixty grand. That's what I heard. Same as a Javelin missile.

Richard I took out a Tali with one of those once. Fucking pink mist, mate, pink mist.

Ali That, my friend, is the power of economics. They pay a farmer ten dollars to take pot shots at you, and you fucking obliterate him with sixty grand's worth of missile.

Roger All's fair, like they say.

Charlie In war maybe. Not in fucking love.

Ali You're not still bleating about your missus, are you?

Charlie Yeah, I am actually. You got a problem with that?

Darren I'm telling you, you're better off without. Mine fucked off before I got back. I wasn't even injured yet. They look nice enough, but they're all fucking nuts. Not that I ever *saw* that much of her. Which was a bit ironic seeing as she worked for Ann Summers. Had sex toys coming out of my ears, but no sex. Three double penetrators but no one to fucking penetrate.

A Nurse enters wearing her prosthetic leg. She carries a clipboard.

Nurse Anyone still want to sign up for kayaking down the Amazon?

David When is it again?

Nurse September.

David Can't. Rowing the Atlantic.

Frank Kilimanjaro.

Nurse Come on, guys, any volunteers?

Ali, John, Roger and Simi exit. The Nurse exits.
   In the brief quiet we hear Chris on the phone.
Darren begins to fall asleep. Leroy enters.

Chris It's blue. On the top. There's a go-faster stripe down the side? No, I'm not a patient here, I'm a . . . I'm a mentor. For the, er, Not Forgotten Association.

Leroy Mentor? More like a fucking mentalist! Weren't doing much mentoring last night were you?

Chris Fuck off.

Chris gives Leroy the finger as he hangs up, looks up another number from his screen and begins to dial.
   Charlie has taken the sock off his stump and is massaging his scar.

Leroy How come your stump's so fucking Gucci?

Charlie Gucci? What's so fucking Gucci about my stump?

Leroy The scar. Yours is well neat. Mine's like a fucking arse.

He rolls up his trouser leg.

Look, it's got bum cheeks and everything. I could fart out of this fucker.

Charlie You should get some ink on that.

He looks at it more closely.

I mean, I was going to make mine a shark's mouth. But that. You're halfway to a whole face there. Or even a knob. Do you still feel yours?

Leroy My knob?

Charlie No! Your legs.

Leroy Yeah. Not always, but sometimes. If I sit on the floor it feels like my legs are going through the floor. It's weird.

Charlie I get this itch in my ankle. The one that isn't there any more? Drives me fucking mad. Feels like my whole leg is in a really thick ski boot.

Chris It's Nike. Yeah, Nike.

Leroy Charlie, you been offered much porn work?

Charlie What?

Leroy Porn. Since you lost your leg? You been offered any work?

Charlie Er, no?

Beat.

Why, have you?

Leroy Yeah. Loads.

Charlie Really?

Leroy Yeah. Must be a double amputee thing, I guess.

Charlie That's sick.

Beat.

You ever do it?

Leroy Went along once. But, nah. Didn't follow through. The chick was proper fat. And she had this weird birthmark.

Charlie Er, right. And of course you're fucking Tom Cruise.

Leroy You'd be surprised. Women love this. They do.

Chris Hello. Is that the White Horse? I was just wondering if you'd found a leg . . . It's blue, on the top. It's got a trainer on it. Nike . . . OK, thanks.

He hangs up.

Charlie Chris, what the fuck are you doing? You sound like Cinderella.

Chris Trying to find my fucking leg, aren't I?

Leroy Where'd you last see it?

Chris In the Black Lion, I think. Yeah.

He points to Frank.

You was drinking out of it!

Frank Was I?

Charlie Actually, now I come to think of it, yeah, you were. Snakebite and black.

Frank Nice.

Chris Yeah, great. But now I've got no fucking leg for the weekend, have I?

Leroy What you doing on there, Frank?

Frank Editing Jonesy's tapes innit.

Charlie Jonesy? 42 Commando? Killed same day as Steve Owens?

Frank Yeah.

Leroy Why you editing them?

Frank His mum found them in his stuff when it was sent back. She wants me to put them on to DVD, so she can watch them. So now I've got to fucking edit them all, haven't I?

Charlie Why?

Frank Cos half of them is him saying he loves his mum, what it's like in Afghan an' that. But then the other half's this stuff –

Frank presses play. The sounds of two people having sex. Frank shows the laptop to Charlie and Chris.

Charlie Jesus fucking Christ!

Leroy She's wearing his beret!

Chris joins them. As one they all turn their heads to the side, until they are horizontal to the screen.

All Fuck!

A Delivery Man enters, holding a pair of mannequin's legs.

Delivery Man Er, anyone know where I'm putting these?

Frank, Charlie, Chris and Leroy all look up at him. For a moment they stare at him, the sound of Jonesy having sex still coming from the computer.

Leroy Are you taking the piss?

Delivery Man Sorry?

Charlie What the fuck?

The Delivery Man looks down at his docket.

Delivery Man This is, er . . .?

A Nurse enters, carrying the body of a mannequin. It wears a Team GB lycra top.

Nurse Yes, it is. Thanks, I'll sign for those. (*To the Soldiers.*) Perhaps we can let Jonesy rest in peace now?

Frank turns off the volume.

(*To the Delivery Man.*) Just through there please, for the Paralympics display. Thanks.

The Delivery Man goes to exit. As they pass Charlie takes one of the legs.

Charlie You won't be needing this. It's for the *Para* Olympics?

The Delivery Man shrugs and exits with just the one leg. Charlie hands the leg to Chris.

Here you go, Cinders. Until you track down your glass slipper.

Chris Fucking great, thanks.

The Nurse enters.

Nurse Corporal Fowler?

Charlie Yes ma'm! You come to take me away from this tea party?

She hands him a package.

Nurse This came for you. (*To all.*) Meds in five minutes!

Ali enters with the rest of the group who left.

Ali Thank fuck for that.

Charlie pulls out a rectangular piece of metal from his package.

Charlie Sweet! Take a look at that, motherfuckers.

He turns the object around to reveal a personalised numberplate. N0 LEG 14.
The group nod in approval.

Roger Herrick 14?

Charlie Yeah.

Richard What you got coming?

Charlie BMW 3 series. Black. If I'd lost a nut or the other leg I'd have gone for a Merc, but you know, needs must.

Ali I swear, it's getting like a footballer's driveway round here. What is it with you lot and the cars?

Leroy Motobility, isn't it? You have that leg off and you'll qualify too.

Ali Don't joke, mate. I've been thinking about it. I mean, I'm still in this wheelchair when other blokes with one leg are up and climbing fucking Everest. I mean, what?

Leroy Just watch out for the small talk, that's all I'd say.

Ali What?

Leroy I'm not kidding. It's the worst thing about it. You wheel into a room and you can bet some old regimental duffer will clock you and think, 'Oh, young bloke, no legs, I'll go and talk to him.' It's like, I just want a drink, or some food but I can't because I'm too busy passing the time of day with Colonel Blimp about having no fucking legs.

Three Nurses enter carrying trays of medication.

Roger Eh up! Make room for the cavalry.

The Nurses begin going about the room, handing out the medication.

Ali *and* **Roger** (*singing*)
And when they were up they were up
And when they were down they were down
And when they were only halfway up –

Darren is woken by the singing.

Darren
They were neither up nor down.

Ali Wa-hey, the Kraken awakes! Welcome back, Sobey, my son!

The Nurses reach the group. As they hand them their medication they begin singing 'The Meds Round'.

All (*sung*)
Codeine, Tramadol, Fentanyl, Oramorph, Paracetamol, MST, Amitriptyline, Diazepam, Mirtazapine, Citalopram, Ranitidine, Omeprazole, Lactulose, Butran, Ibuprofen, Venlafaxine. Co-codamol.

The lights fade down on the repeating song.

SCENE SIX – SOMEONE TO HOLD

Lights up on a Psychologist talking to Charlie. As they talk the silhouette of a Vallon man sweeping for IEDs is seen upstage.

Psychologist . . . Severe allergic reactions: disorientation; excessive sweating; fainting; fast or irregular heartbeat; fever; hallucinations; loss of coordination; mental or mood changes, agitation, depression, red, swollen, blistered, or peeling skin, and . . . seizures.

Charlie Severe nausea? Vomiting; diarrhoea; headaches; suicidal thoughts – cos I need more of those, right? – Loss of appetite; tiredness; weakness; pale shit and dark piss.

Beat.

And I mean, that's just the Tramadol. Wait till you hear about the Venlafaxine –

Psychologist It's OK, Charlie. I see your point. The meds aren't helping?

Charlie No. The drugs, as the song says, don't fucking work. I mean, yeah, they *work*, but at the same time they mess everything up.

Psychologist Like?

Charlie Sleep. Attention. Anger. Sex.

Psychologist How are things with Lauren?

Beat.

Charlie I don't know. Answer me this, Doc? How can you be angry at someone for loving you too much? She'll try and help me, or cuddle me – oh, yeah, cuddling, that's the worst – and I'll be like, 'Get the fuck off me!'

Psychologist You've lost interest in sex?

Charlie No. Yes. I mean . . . you get back and you *think* what you want is a slut. It is. You think you'll want to do all that stuff you've been dreaming about doing for six fucking months in the desert. But when you *do* get back, you don't. You don't. The juices aren't flowing. Not the *actual* juices, no problem there – but you know, the metaphorical ones. You want something else instead.

Psychologist And what's that? What do you want?

Charlie Exactly what she's offering. That closeness, the contact. But when she does. There's this fucking distance and I just want to be alone. On my own.

Chris enters and approaches the Psychologist.

Chris She doesn't understand. She thinks I'm a lazy bastard. I know she does. She gives me these fucking chores, these lists. And then the meds knock me out. And what the kids say. That's the worst. 'Daddy, are you drunk?' 'Why is Daddy sleeping all the time?'

Psychologist Have you tried explaining things to them?

David Like what? How every time I see them I think of those kids in Afghan? No. I've put my bed in the back room now. So they don't have to see me like this.

Psychologist And your wife? How's she coping?

Chris Don't get me wrong. I know how hard it's been for her. They've all had to get on without me. And that's part of the problem – they've got their own routines now. Without me. They live without me.

Beat.

Do you know what she said the other day? 'Chris didn't come back.' That's what she said. 'The Chris that went away hasn't come back.' And in a way she's right. She is.

Frank enters and approaches the Psychologist.

Frank I'll just go out on the piss all day. Don't give a fuck, then I'll get wound up by something small and I'll just want to smash something up. Or someone.

Psychologist Only when you drink?

Frank Well, the drink makes it worse. The anger's there all the time. And these images. Like, I don't fucking know. When an IED blew my mate's hands off. The look in his eyes. That kind of thing.

Psychologist You're on probation now, right?

Frank Yeah. But they said if I come and talk to you, it'll keep me out of prison.

Psychologist Does that worry Michelle? You going away again? Doing time?

Frank Yeah, yeah, it does.

Beat.

I don't know. When she's talking to me. When I can't be near her. I just want to go back there, get vengeance on the fuckers who done this to me. It's like . . . it's like there's hatred running through my whole body. But I do love her. I do.

Chris She's right. She is.

Charlie She's pretty amazing, Doc. I mean, I know she's my solution. But I'm fucking it up. And it's like I can't stop.

As he continues the three women, Lauren, Marie and Michelle (carrying a child) enter and come to stand beside the three men.

It's like I really, really want to square this one away but I can't. It's a whole second tour, Doc. It is. The one no one tells you about. I mean, I'll storm a fucking compound tomorrow. Even with one fucking leg. But *this* tour. I'm outnumbered. You take meds for the pain, then meds for the meds. Then every time you close your eyes . . .

The Psychologist exits.

And the casualties. That's what's so fucked up. They're the very people you always said you'd fight for. The ones you said you'd protect. The ones you love.

Charlie reaches a hand out towards Lauren. She takes off her engagement ring and places it in his palm, then turns away.

Chris reaches towards Marie. She stares at him as if she doesn't know him, then places a child's toy in his hand before turning away.

69

Frank reaches towards Michelle. She looks at the baby, then at him, then turns away.

The three women exit, followed by Chris and Frank.

Music: 'Someone to Hold' by Anthony and the Johnsons.

Chris and Leroy enter to join Charlie in a wheelchair dance. The three women enter to join them.

As the dancers exit John appears in close-up, projected on the screen.

John (*on screen*) My mum, bless her, she quit her job to stay with me. She'd be trying to care for me, and I'd be like, really snappy, telling her to fuck off, go away. Then straight away I'd think, 'Why did I do that?' It's weird, you want it, you do. But then you'll be a twat, and tell them to fuck off. It's like being two people. But she's amazing, she is. She's always been there when I needed her. I'd go out on the piss, and she'd find me later, in her kitchen, fucking laughing at YouTube clips of IEDs. Just going crazy. Then ten minutes later, I'd be in her arms, crying. She's had to put up with so much. But she's always supported me, always.

Fade to black.

SCENE SEVEN – ENEMY TERRITORY

Speeches by Daniel and Chris are projected on to the stage.

Daniel How I think of it is, I've got my old brain, and my new brain. My old brain was the one that evolved for the first thirty-eight years of my life. It was me. My new brain, that's the one I was given when I was blown up. I mean, in an instant I became a different person. And people don't always understand. When I say my brain hurts, or I have trouble thinking, or that I get really tired they'll say, 'Oh yeah, I get that sometimes too.' It's frustrating, because I don't like the new me. I don't always recognise myself, and they just don't understand.

Chris I call it 'stump jump', these sudden spasms and shocks, like I've touched a car battery with the end of my stump. I've found vodka and Ibuprofen's a good cure for that. But then there's the phantom pain too – 10,000 volts going through legs you don't have. A lit match stuck under my toenail, burning for days. It's the frustration that breeds the anger though, as much as the pain. When I first got home from the hospital I tried to build a kennel for my dog. A flat-pack thing it was, but I couldn't fucking do it could I? Couldn't even build a fucking kennel. I ended up taking a hammer to it in the end, smashed it to pieces all over the lawn.

Lights come up to reveal Charlie, wearing his prosthetic and a pair of shorts.

Charlie You know what my nickname was in the Corps? Foxtrot. And no, not for my fancy fucking footwork either. Charlie Fowler. C.F. – in NATO phonetics, 'Charlie Foxtrot'. In Army and Navy slang – 'Clusterfuck: a situation disintegrating in every direction at once.' I won't lie to you, for a while there, after this happened, I *became* my nickname.

I mean, I was a fucking mess. And I wasn't alone. There's the denial phase, the 'sitting on your ass playing Xbox, pissing everyone off' phase, the meds, the pain . . . But we're soldiers, you know. What do they teach us in training? Adapt and overcome. And that's what you do, eventually.

Beat.

In the end, for me, there were two things that really made that happen. The first was realising that just like

71

you fight for your mates, your boys, out there, on the ground, so you can fight for them here too. It might be just a phone call, an email, dropping round. But you can look out for each other *here* just like you did on tour. I mean, whenever we pushed into new areas in Afghan, we went as a patrol, didn't we? And it's the same here.

When we push into that uncharted territory, as much as possible, we do so *together*.

Oh, yeah, the second thing? Well . . . actually, you know what? You're about to hear about that now anyway.

As Charlie walks upstage lights come up to reveal a lapdancing club. Two backlit screens show the silhouettes of two Dancers. A Waitress is taking a drinks order from two Businessmen. Roger, Ali, John, Simi and Darren all enter to join Charlie.

Ali Charlie Boy! What's your poison?

Charlie Beer. Thanks, man.

Richard Are we all here?

Daniel Er, yeah. Aren't we? I thought I counted everyone off . . .

Ali Jesus! Who put the guy with the neuro injury in charge of numbers?

Daniel I could have sworn . . .

Leroy enters.

Leroy Great, thanks for that, lads. Had to be carried up by old Tweedledee and Tweedledum out there, didn't I?

The two Dancers come out from behind the screen and begin to mingle among the Soldiers as the Waitress takes drinks orders.

Dancer 1 Hello, love. You interested in a private dance?

Leroy Er, yeah, I guess so. Is it a lapdance?

She looks at his legs.

Dancer 1 Well, it's hardly going to be a waltz, is it, darling? Yes, it's a lapdance.

Leroy That's lucky, cos a lap's all I got!

Leroy and Dancer 1 go behind the screens.

Ali All right, darling?

Waitress Evening, sir.

Ali You know what a fat penguin does?

Waitress I'm sorry?

Ali Breaks the ice! Get it? Breaks the ice . . .

The two Businessmen approach Charlie and Chris.

Businessman 1 All right, lads? Having a good night?

Businessman 2 Are you all, er, veterans, then? Is that it?

Charlie Well, some of us are still serving. We're soldiers but, yeah.

Businessman 1 Well, I think you do a fantastic job. Really. People don't recognise it enough.

Businessman 2 I've got a friend who was in the Army.

Charlie Right. Great.

Businessman 1 Look, will you let us get you all a round. Please. It would be our pleasure.

Charlie No, honestly, you're all right, mate.

Ali Shut up, Charlie. Jack and Coke please, mate, cheers!

Businessman 2 Waitress! Waitress! A round for these lads, please. On us.

Businessman 1 So, have you been overseas?

Charlie Yeah.

Chris Yeah.

Businessman 2 Iraq, was it?

Chris Afghan.

Businessman 1 Wow. Really? So you've seen some action then?

Charlie looks at their missing legs.

Charlie Er, yeah? A bit.

Chris Some.

Businessman 2 Did you kill any?

Charlie Sorry?

Businessman 1 I think what he's asking is whether you killed anyone over there?

Beat.

Did you?

Charlie Er, I don't really want to –

Businessman 2 How many? Do you know?

Chris Look –

Businessman 1 I imagine it'd be hard to tell? From what I hear you don't often see them, do you?

Roger joins the group.

Roger Look, mate, thanks for the drinks and everything, but do you mind not asking those kind of questions?

Businessman 2 Oh. Oh, I'm sorry.

Businessman 1 We didn't mean to cause offence. Sorry.

Businessman 2 Are you with them too?

Roger 'Them'? Who the fuck is 'them'?

Businessman 2 The soldiers.

Roger Yeah. I am.

Businessman 2 So . . . I mean, sorry, but what's wrong with you?

Roger I don't know, I broke my back in two places, had discs at C4 and C5 replaced, I'm addicted to meds and sometimes the pain is so bad I collapse and piss myself in public. What's wrong with you?

Darren and John come over.

John All right, Rog, take it easy.

The Businessmen back off.

Businessman 2 Right. OK. Fine.

Roger Prick.

Dancer 2 approaches Charlie. She wears a nurse's outfit.

Dancer 2 Hello, it's Charlie, isn't it?

Charlie Oh God, you know my name. Have I really been here that much?

Dancer 2 Once or twice. Look, would you like a private dance?

Charlie Er, thanks, but I'm fine. Thanks.

Dancer 2 Really? Even if I say please?

Charlie Well, no. Honestly, that's sweet, but . . .

Businessman 1 Take the dance. It's on us. Please.

Ali If you don't want it, Charlie, I'll have it!

Dancer 2 Please?

Charlie OK, OK, I'll have the dance.

The screens are moved to isolate Charlie and Dancer 2.

Look, I'll be honest, I'm not really in the mood for this.

Dancer 2 It's all right. I didn't really want to give you a dance.

Charlie Oh. Then why –?

Dancer 2 Because I wanted to give you something else.

Charlie Oh, right. Well, Jesus. That's really kind of you. I mean, I know everyone's getting into this 'help for heroes' stuff, but –

Dancer 2 Who's Lauren?

Beat.

Charlie Sorry?

Dancer 2 Lauren? Who is she?

Charlie How do you know –?

Dancer 2 When you've been in before. When you get drunk. You start talking about her. A lot.

Charlie I do? Yeah, I guess that happens.

Dancer 2 And that tat on your arm. I'm guessing it used to say her name?

Charlie Yeah. Yeah, it did. Before the frag and the scars fucked it up. Guess I should have known then, eh?

Dancer 2 Known what?

Charlie She's my fiancée . . . She *was* my fiancée.

Dancer 2 Oh. Bollocks. I'm sorry.

Charlie Not your fault. Not hers either. All mine.

Dancer 2 I guess you might not want this now then.

Charlie Want what?

Dancer 2 This.

She hands him a folded piece of paper.

Charlie What is it?

Dancer 2 Well, I've seen you've all got tattoos. You all seem to like tats.

Charlie Yeah, everyone likes a bit of ink.

Dancer 2 So I designed a new one for you. I've gone back to college. It's meant to be, well, I thought you might like a new one.

Charlie 'Lauren'.

Dancer 2 Yeah, but I understand if –

Charlie It's beautiful.

Dancer 2 You can change the words underneath if you want. And the name now, I guess!

Charlie 'But love survives the venom of the snake.'

Dancer 2 It's from this poem we're studying. It's by a soldier, but, like I said –

Charlie It's perfect. Thank you.

Beat.

Dancer 2 Is it really over?

Charlie I don't know.

Dancer 2 Cos the way you talk about her. When –

Charlie I know. I know.

Dancer 2 Look, I'm going to have to go. The manager gets in a right strop if we're in here too long. But, well, like I said. I wanted to give you something. Sorry if it's –

Charlie I meant what I said. It's perfect. Thank you.

She leans in and gives him a peck on the cheek, then exits.
The lights stay up on Charlie.

SCENE EIGHT – LEAVING

Charlie 'But love survives the venom of the snake.'
When you're discharged from the services one of the last things you do is hand over your ID. Your identity. It's a death, of sorts. At least, it certainly feels like a kind of grief, afterwards. A mourning. For the loss of that bond. For the family you'd joined, lived with, fought with, but are now being asked to leave.

It feels sudden. One day you're in. The next you're out. But it isn't. It's a slow process. A process of departure. And that's one of the problems. It takes seconds to hand over that ID. But it can take years to remove the uniform.

We do have to take it off though, one day. The stories of our injuries all began with an engagement of some kind. A contact. And they're only going to be brought to an end with another kind of contact. Another kind of engagement –

He looks at the tattoo design.

– or re-engagement. But you can't do that if you're still wearing your uniform.

It's OK though. Because it isn't just about leaving, is it? It's about joining too, right? I mean all of us here, yeah, we're leaving the services, but we're also joining the oldest regiment there is. The regiment of the wounded.

78

It's a regiment with an illustrious history that goes back to the earliest days of mankind. You might not be familiar with all of its victories, but believe me it has thousands to its name. Millions. And it's winning them every day. In hospitals, on the streets, in bedrooms and living rooms.

He taps his head.

In here.

The rest of the cast enter upstage and begin walking downstage to join Charlie.

The regimental rank and file are recruited from all over the world. Britain. America. Africa. Iraq. Afghanistan. Men. Women. Children. And it's growing. Even now, as we speak, it's growing. And until we stop fighting, it's going to keep on growing. And it's deploying too. Every day. Not to a battlefield, or to a base. But to you. To out there. We've all been training for that deployment. We've been getting ready, and now we are ready. So we hope you are too. Because we don't live in two worlds, do we? We live in one.

Beat.

And don't you ever forget it.

Fade to black.

In Hospital: Poona (1)

ALUN LEWIS

Last night I did not fight for sleep
But lay awake from midnight while the world
Turned its slow features to the moving deep
Of darkness, till I knew that you were furled,

Beloved, in the same dark watch as I.
And sixty degrees of longitude beside
Vanished as though a swan in ecstasy
Had spanned the distance from your sleeping side.

And like to swan or moon the whole of Wales
Glided within the parish of my care:
I saw the green tide leap on Cardigan,
Your red yacht riding like a legend there,

And the great mountains Dafydd and Llewelyn,
Plynlimmon, Cader Idris and Eryri
Threshing the darkness back from head and fin,
And also the small nameless mining valley

Whose slopes are scratched with streets and
    sprawling graves
Dark in the lap of firwoods and great boulders
Where you lay waiting, listening to the waves –
My hot hands touched your white despondent shoulders

– And then ten thousand miles of daylight grew
Between us, and I heard the wild daws crake
In India's starving throat; whereat I knew
That Time upon the heart can break
But love survives the venom of the snake.

Reprinted by kind permission of the author and publisher
from Alun Lewis, *Collected Poems* (Seren, 1994)

GLOSSARY

AGC	*Adjutant General's Corps*
ANA	*Afghan National Army*
BLESMA	*British Limbless Ex Service Men's Association*
bluey	*airmail letter*
CamelBak	*water-bottle*
ECM	*Electronic Countermeasure System*
FOB	*Forward Operating Base*
GPMG	*General Purpose Machine Gun*
Hesco block	*fortification device*
IED	*Improvised Explosive Device*
medevac	*medical evacuation*
oppo	*best friend*
OPTAG	*Operational Training and Advisory Group*
Osprey	*body armour*
PB	*Patrol Base*
Pinzgauer	*all-terrain vehicle*
PRR	*Personal Role Radio*
PRU	*Personnel Recovery Unit*
2PWRR	*Second Battalion, The Princess of Wales's Royal Regiment*
QE Nurses	*Queen Elizabeth Military Hospital Nurses*
QRF	*Quick Reaction Force*
RPG	*Rocket-Propelled Grenade*
sangar duty	*guard duty (from a watch tower)*
Snatch	*Protected Patrol Vehicle*
terp	*interpreter*
TLA	*Three-Letter Acronym*
UGL	*Underslung Grenade Launcher*
Wimik (WMIK)	*armoured military vehicle*